Saddam's Attacks on America: 1993; September 11, 2001; and the Anthrax Attacks

Saddam's Attacks on America: 1993; September 11, 2001; and the Anthrax Attacks

◆

A freewheeling and hard-hitting commentary on the life-threatening problems facing America and the prescription for their cure.

Dr. Hugh Cort III.

iUniverse, Inc.

New York Lincoln Shanghai

Saddam's Attacks on America: 1993; September 11, 2001; and the Anthrax Attacks
A freewheeling and hard-hitting commentary on the life-threatening problems facing America and the prescription for their cure.

iUniverse, Inc.

For information address:
iUniverse, Inc.
2021 Pine Lake Road, Suite 100
Lincoln, NE 68512
www.iuniverse.com

ISBN: 0-595-31585-2

Printed in the United States of America

To my father, Captain Hugh Cort Jr., who served with the 70th Tank Battalion and was wounded in action in the Korean War, and my grandfather, General Hugh Cort, General in World War II, who taught me what courage is,

To my wife, Deborah, and my mother, Violet, who always encouraged me,

To the modern day patriots, and to all patriots—past, present, and future—that made and make and will continue to make America great,

To the victims of terror everywhere, and their families, and to our courageous troops on the front line in the War Against Terror.

Essay by my mother, Violet Price Cort, in 1953

I have a shining silver dollar in my purse of memories. When my husband was stationed with a battalion of an Armored Cavalry regiment in Western Germany we lived in a small Bavarian town named Amberg. Picturesque and charming, it is surrounded by a thick wall of quaint dwelling places; opening secretively onto the inside of the town, they can hardly be called houses.

On a gray afternoon I stood with a German friend and my two-year-old son, awaiting the parade with which the American battalion was celebrating Armed Forces Day. All the vehicles that could run were to circle the old walled town on the modern, black-topped road called the Kaiser-Wilhem Ring.

The dark clouds lowered menacingly, the wind was biting, and the dwellings in the wall were bleak despite their red-tiled roofs. A few cars went by, a few people hurried along under the bare-leaved trees of the Kaiser-Wilhem promenade. There was no warning that something special was about to happen for me.

The actual incident was brief. The first jeep clattered around the corner carrying a short standard from which floated the American Flag. I became suddenly homesick, filled with longing for my family's home in the States. Then the tanks came. They were monsters, giants, shapes from another world. They were magnificent. Pride took the place of nostalgia; pride in my husband's work, pride in my son, now perched on my arm, watching for Daddy, pride in those fearsome tanks.

It was quickly over. We saw Daddy; he saw us, and waved. The thundering tanks disappeared around the curve of the Ring, and the noise faded on the cold air. We turned and trudged up the hill toward our house on Steingutstrasse. That ancient town and those roaring tanks seem far away now, but I still have my coin, my rare silver dollar.

May 12, 2004

Dear Dr. Cort:

Michael Reagan asked that I thank you for your thoughtful book regarding the terrorist threat faced by America. You are to be congratulated for your hard work in putting together such an impressive document.

With best regards,

Sincerely yours,

William Perry Pendley
President and Chief Legal Officer

Contents

Acknowledgments

I give thanks to my long-suffering typist, Tonya Swain, who has had to put up with my obsessive-compulsive focus on details of punctuation and grammar (Dear Reader, please note that at times I have employed poetic license in some of my syntax!) Tonya's hard work and patience has been a great blessing, and she is greatly appreciated.

I will now thank the many wonderful people in TV, press, radio, and books who have helped shape my views of the world.

I give thanks to the brilliant cable news shows, FOX and MSNBC, that give us the truth and fair and balanced reporting that is so sadly lacking in the mainstream (liberal) media.

I give thanks to Sean Hannity for all the insights and information on his dynamic FOX TV show, Hannity and Colmes, and his excellent book, the benchmark and gold standard <u>Let Freedom Ring</u>.

I give thanks to Michael Savage and his incisive book, <u>Savage Nation</u>.

I thank Newt Gingrich, for his insight, hard work, and courage.

I thank Rush Limbaugh for his pioneering work in conservative talk radio that helped get this country headed in the right direction.

I thank Laura Ingraham for her intellectual strength and her clear perception of how things really are.

I thank conservative talk radio show hosts all across America.

I thank the <u>National Enquirer</u> for their in-depth research and coverage that so often beats the mainstream press to the punch.

I thank Michael Ledeen for his excellent book, <u>The Terror Masters</u>.

I thank Joe Scarborough for his terrific news and commentary show, <u>Scarbor-ough Country</u>.

I thank Bill O'Reilly for his great show and crisp, logical thinking.

I thank Ann Coulter for her courage and intelligence and her excellent books.

I thank Pat Robertson and Jerry Falwell and Hal Lindsey for their great spiritual guidance and leadership.

I thank Paul and Jan Crouch for starting up the greatest TV station and most important TV station in the world, Trinity Broadcasting Network (TBN).

And finally, I thank God, for giving us America, and for giving the American Dream to the world.

Prologue

This book is dedicated to all patriots, past, present, and future, and especially to the modern day patriots of America—Ronald Reagan, George H.W. Bush, George W. Bush, Rush Limbaugh, Newt Gingrich, Sean Hannity, Joe Scarborough, Michael Savage, Ann Coulter, Michael Ledeen, Bill O'Reilly, Laura Ingraham, Pat Robertson, Jerry Falwell, Hal Lindsey, Paul and Jan Crouch, and many others, especially the brave American men and women in our armed forces who fought and died and are fighting and dying this day in Afghanistan and Iraq so that terrorists and madmen will not be able to hurt our country again, not only with hijacked airplanes but also with chemical and biological and <u>nuclear</u> weapons, and also let us not forget the brave firefighters and policemen of New York City who gave their lives on September 11 so that others might live. And also let us praise the conservative radio talk shows all across America, and Fox News, and MSNBC, for bringing the truth to America, despite the best efforts of the liberal media to suppress the truth and distort it. And finally, let us always remember the victims of terror everywhere, and their families, and may God comfort them in their grief, and give them His peace, which passes all understanding.

The liberals call the patriots mentioned above "the radical right" but in actual truth they are exactly in the center of where America needs to be, and the liberal left is truly "out in left field." The liberal left has left America and the values that uphold us. If we follow the liberal left we will be like the lemmings that mindlessly follow their leaders off the cliff in a mass suicide jump into the sea.

Finally, we must thoroughly castigate the pathetic Democrat "leaders" (losers) that are "running" for the Democrat nomination for the presidential race of 2004. To me, it appears they are not only floundering all over the place, shooting themselves in the feet with their ridiculous slander of President Bush, sure to lose votes and lose <u>big</u> in the 2004 election, but they are bordering on treason with their over-the-top criticism, and they are totally wrong in criticizing George Bush for solving a large part of the terror problem by destroying the al-Qaida training grounds in Afghanistan and by destroying the regime of Saddam Hussein, who was about to get nuclear weapons and cause the terrorist movement to go nuclear. What further is galling about the Democrats is that not only do they bash Bush for helping solve the terrorist problem, they are the ones who helped create the security lapses that lead to the problem in the first place and September 11, by Clinton and Gore's pathetic and apathetic response over <u>eight</u> years of terrorist attacks on U.S. interests (remember that Sudan, <u>several</u> times tried to give Osama bin Laden over to U.S. Custody but Clinton <u>turned them down</u> each time, [see Sean Hannity's book <u>Let Freedom Ring</u> pages 16—20] even though Clinton knew Osama was the greatest single financier of terrorist projects in the world). And Richard Miniter in his new book <u>Losing Bin Laden</u> says Clinton and Gore had <u>twelve</u> chances to capture or kill bin Laden and they blew it. So the Democrat losers running for their party's 2004 presidential nomination are not only trying to lead America in the wrong direction, they are also very disrespectful of our Commander-in-Chief. Can you imagine politicians bashing Franklin Delano Roosevelt and the war effort in World War II after Pearl Harbor? It is a <u>travesty</u> that the Democrats are bashing Bush for going to war on terror in Afghanistan and Iraq after September 11.

The Democrats, with their constant carping and criticism, are hurting the morale of our troops, and are aiding and abetting the terrorists whose goal it is to get the United States out of Iraq so they can take over and make it a terrorist paradise. The Democrats are indirectly (or, in Michael Moore's case, directly) encouraging the terrorists to kill our troops and innocent Iraqis. It is one thing to propose alternative ideas, but the Democrats have gone way too far in their vicious bashing of President Bush and the war on terror. Let us bash and <u>thrash</u> the <u>Democrats</u> in the elections of 2004, and give them the thrashing they deserve.

Chapter I

◆

Why I dislike the Democratic "Leadership" (Losership) and Their Mouthpiece, the Liberal Media

Let me try to explain why I dislike the Democrat leaders (losers) so much. I don't dislike regular Democrat voters; in fact many of my friends consider themselves Democrats. I share many of my Democrat friends' what I call "good" liberal values, like concern for the environment, concern for education, and concern for the poor. What I don't like are the Democrat leaders who have led the Democrat party far to the liberal left, far away from the party of FDR. They are determinedly for abortion, and totally soft on defense, they are against fighting our enemies who seek to destroy us, they want to tax and spend us to death, they want to control us with their stifling "politically correct" ways, they are soft on crime and they want to ruin our morals and our foundation of God and family.

I merely disagreed with the Democratic leadership before September 11th happened. When September 11th happened, I realized the Democrats were to blame for a great part of the security lapses and cultural decay that led to September 11. (Remember when Hilary Clinton tried to give a speech to the firefighters and police of New York City and they booed her because her husband had many chances to get Osama before September 11, and he let America down because of his failure to act against terror!) How come the liberal media tried to gloss this over and barely reported it? Because they love Hilary and Bill and the Democrat liberal left.

So when September 11 happened, my disagreement with the Democrat leadership turned into dislike and rightfully so. When you see a people that you love, the American people, being led over a cliff to destruction, and you realize that if the Democrats get elected in 2004 or 2008 or 2012 that they will lead the country to <u>slaughter</u>, that their failed policies will lead to destruction of America's cities by nuclear blasts and that <u>millions</u> will die and that September 11, horrible as it was, will pale in comparison, you will naturally dislike such Democratic leadership with all your heart, even as the British in World War II came to despise Neville Chamberlain for his cowardly appeasement of Hitler. And furthermore, now we have learned, it was Neville Chamberlain's sacrifice of Czechoslovakia to appease Hitler that gave Czechoslovakia's tanks and weapons factories to Germany, which allowed them to <u>quickly invade</u> Poland and France. We must re-elect George W. Bush in 2004 and Republicans in 2008 and 2012, just as Britain elected Churchill in World War II. If we elect a Democrat president, we are doomed.

In this book I will demonstrate the <u>clear</u> link between Saddam Hussein, Osama bin Laden and al-Qaida, and their joint attacks on the U.S. in the first World Trade Center bombing in 1993, the destruction of the World Trade Center and the attack on the Pentagon on September 11, 2001, and the anthrax letter attacks of October 2001. We will see how Saddam, his fiendishly evil ego infuriated by America kicking him out of Kuwait in 1991, instigated and used Osama bin Laden and al-Qaida as his hit men to get revenge on America, and how George W. Bush and Tony Blair are true heroes forever for destroying Saddam <u>before</u> he got nuclear weapons (and he was very close to getting them!), because Saddam would have given nuclear weapons to terrorists to use on the U.S., and he would also have used them to re-invade Kuwait, and also Saudi Arabia and eventually the whole Persian Gulf. Several defectors have said Saddam had as many as six hidden nuclear development sites in Iraq. When Iraq is stabilized, their scientists will be able to tell us about his nuclear program. And also Saddam, who already tried to get illegal missiles from North Korea, could have eventually purchased a nuclear bomb from North Korea. We know North Korea illegally gave Libya uranium for its nuclear program.

This will show that the pathetic Democrats who are bashing Bush for destroying Saddam should be tarred and feathered and run out of town on a rail, or the political equivalent of that which is to be thoroughly trounced in the 2004 election. We need to send a powerful message to the Democrats that they are trying to lead the country in the <u>totally</u> wrong direction, and that we are not going to listen to their garbage any more.

Even more importantly than whipping the Democrats in 2004 and 2008 and 2012, this book will show some of the root causes of why we got hit in 2001, and will show some ways we can avoid being hit again. My fear is that America will <u>not</u> learn enough from September 11, and we may elect a Democrat president in 2004, 2008 or 2012, and we may persist in the wrong actions, and we will definitely incur the wrath of God and we will see New York and Washington D.C. and Los Angeles and Chicago go up in nuclear mushroom clouds. Even then God may give us another chance to change our ways—if we follow Him, we will be blessed and He will give us victory over the terrorists. If we do not follow Him, we will be destroyed. The choice is ours.

I must here say a word about the "fifth column"—a term which refers to a treasonous, additional arm of the enemy in wartime—which today is unquestionably the liberal left media. These leftist, biased TV stations and newspapers (For example the <u>New York Times</u> fiction newspaper—"We make up the news to fit our liberal agenda") often give misleading news and, most importantly, <u>leave out</u> the most pertinent news because it doesn't fit their propagandist agenda. As one of Pat Robertson's fine news announcers, Lee Webb, says, "The bias of the liberal left media is not so much in what they print but in the stories they purposely <u>fail</u> to print."

Here is one of the biggest stories ever—that the press and media have <u>purposefully</u> ignored the truth that Saddam and al-Qaida have been linked together, and have tried to fool the public into thinking there is no link! They have ignored the truth of Stephen Hayes' article, "Case Closed," in the November 24, 2003 issue of <u>The Weekly Standard</u>, detailing "The U.S. Government's secret evidence of cooperation between Saddam Hussein and Osama bin Laden."

The liberal media was against the war in Iraq because it would make the Republicans look strong and also because they failed to accurately assess the danger Saddam posed to America and also because they are afraid to act decisively. The pathetic Democratic leadership is <u>so frustrated</u> that Bush and the Republicans are looking good in the war against terror and have gained control for the first time of the Senate, the House, and the White House in fifty years, since the time of Republican control under the great Dwight Eisenhower (I Like Ike!) that the Democrats will cheat, steal, lie, and possibly even kill to get back their control (witness the Democrats' <u>blatant cheating</u> in their promotion of Lautenberg for Senate in New Jersey even though this was clearly <u>in violation</u> of election rules!)—and witness the obscene calumny of Ted Kennedy, who has done more to ruin America than any one man in history except Bill Clinton, who claims President Bush went to war against Iraq to increase the clout of the Republican Party. Ted, you are so wrong! President Bush went to war against Iraq to stop Saddam Hussein before he got nukes and could give them to his <u>close</u> buddies Osama bin Laden and al-Qaida to blow up Manhattan and Washington D.C. and Philly and Chicago and L.A! Ted Kennedy's charges against George Bush are <u>treasonous</u>, and are the equivalent of a Senator in World War II accusing FDR of waging war against the Germans in order to further the Democrats' hold on power! What garbage! Ted Kennedy, and his partner-in-crime, Bill Clinton, belong in the trash can of history for their degradation of America. I can't believe the nerve Ted Kennedy has calling President Bush's war on the horrible terrorist Saddam Hussein a "fraud." If anyone is a fraud, it is Ted Kennedy.

The reason I am bringing up liberal media spin is because many times the media has tried to "discredit" reports that Saddam Hussein was linked with Osama bin Laden and al-Qaida terrorists. Stephen Hayes, the brilliant staff writer at The Weekly Standard, whose work should be on the front page of every paper in America, and who truly deserves the Pulitzer Prize, writes in his article in the June 28, 2004 issue entitled "There They Go Again" "the 9/11 Commission and the media refuse to see the ties between Saddam Hussein and al Qaeda." He goes on to say "The U.S. Intelligence Community has long believed that Saddam was willing to use Islamic militants—including al Qaeda—to exact revenge on the United States for his humiliating defeat in the first Gulf War." Hayes continues, "Saddam offered bin Laden safe haven in Iraq in late 1998 or early 1999." Hayes also gives several pages documenting Mohammed Atta's trips to Prague as confirmed by five senior Czech officials, and he blasts the 9/11 Commission's erroneous and truly ridiculous assertion that Atta could not have made one of his several trips, the April 2001 trip, because his cell phone was used from Florida to call other Florida phone numbers in April. Doesn't it occur to the 9/11 Commission that Atta left his cell phone behind with his terrorist buddies when he went to Europe, especially since that cell phone doesn't work in Europe, and it was his terrorist buddies who made the Florida calls while Atta was in Prague? The 9/11 Commission members are no super sleuths! They make Inspector Closseau look like Sherlock Holmes! As Hayes writes, "It is entirely possible that Atta would leave his cell phone behind if he left the country. In any case, hijackers are known to have shared cell phones." The reason why the media doesn't want to see a link between Saddam and September 11 is because they did not want war with Iraq because

1. they didn't want the Republicans to increase in power as the party that fights terrorists

2. they are chicken-hearted Neville Chamberlain appeasers who bury their heads in the sand rather than deal with the death threat that Saddam posed since he was right on the verge of getting nukes (anyone who thinks Saddam did not have a nuclear program and was not actively seeking nuclear weapons is in total denial)

3. they want to be in some namby-pamby nebulous impractical and essentially anti-U.S. "world community" and they support the French who put their selfish interest of Iraqi oil contracts ahead of world peace and security, and the United Nations which is comprised mostly of dictatorships and has a clear anti-U.S. bias.

Now the Democrats and their propaganda mouthpiece, the liberal media, are doing everything they can to discredit Bush and the war on Iraq—anything—lie, calumny, fraud—anything to get their power back. They are like Gollum and the evil Sauron of Mordor screaming and scheming to get the power of the ring! And, like all evil, they must be stopped.

There is so much circumstantial and direct evidence that links Saddam and September 11 that you would have to be an ostrich with your head in the sand to ignore it—yet this is what the Dems and the liberal media are doing! Fortunately the American people have a lot of common sense and they are not fooled by the media and they know that Saddam was behind September 11! Seventy percent of Americans are not wrong! The liberals are wrong!

Every time evidence shows up linking Saddam to al-Qaida and September 11, and showing Saddam was very close to getting nukes, the press tries to discredit it falsely, saying, "Well this source says it wasn't true, or this source says it was fabricated." I say, look at the evidence. Then look at the people who try to discredit the evidence. Then you will see that the evidence, both circumstantial and direct, definitely connects Saddam with the first bombing of the World Trade Center in 1993, the destruction of the World Trade Center September 11, 2001 and the attack on the Pentagon and the attempted attack on the Capitol (the United Airlines Flight 93 that our heroic passengers stopped) and possibly an attempted attack on the White House. (It is possible there was a fifth plane that was grounded before it could be hijacked to hit the White House). The evidence also links Saddam to the anthrax attacks. Also the evidence shows that Saddam did import uranium yellowcake illegally from Africa. British Intelligence stands by their statement that Saddam obtained yellowcake uranium from Niger. There was a forged document that of course can no longer be considered evidence. However there are several more pieces of evidence that do show that Saddam obtained uranium from Africa, which is why the British stand by their statement. There is very little security in Niger where yellowcake uranium is mined and transported. A person can easily go up to the driver of a truck with yellowcake and give the driver a hundred dollars and he will throw off a few bricks of yellowcake. So yellowcake uranium is not hard to find or obtain in Niger.

The British have documented reports that Iraqi villagers once stole several large vats containing yellowcake uranium. They used the vats as water containers (not realizing the vats were possibly radioactive) and dumped the yellowcake on the ground. The evidence also shows that Saddam was <u>very close</u> to getting nuclear weapons, and that he not only had al-Samood missiles that go 93 miles, but also had al-Hussein missiles that go 400 miles! If Saddam got nukes, and gave them to terrorists to use on our cities, and put them on warheads to wipe out Tel Aviv and Riyadh if we opposed a new conquest by him of Kuwait and Saudi Arabia, we would be facing disaster. As Congressman Terry Everett of Alabama says in his October 2003 newsletter, Iraq was not only "harboring and assisting al-Qaida, it was also actively working on programs to generate weapons of mass destruction that could have been used by both the Iraqi regime as well as al-Qaida terrorists."

Remember, some evidence in the intelligence world is sometimes murky, sometimes cloudy, sometimes bits and pieces, and at times we only see the tip of the iceberg threatening ominously, while the bulk of the iceberg is unseen below the surface, waiting to sink the next Titanic. But when you put the whole picture together, all the bits and pieces, and connect the dots, the awesome and terrifying truth emerges that Saddam instigated Osama and al-Qaida to destroy the World Trade Center on September 11, and he was inches away from getting nukes and giving them to al-Qaida to blow up all of New York City and Washington D.C. and Los Angeles and Chicago, and if George W. Bush and Tony Blair hadn't courageously defied all sorts of ridiculous opposition from Democrats, the media, the U.N., the European Union and Hollywood, and courageously stopped Saddam as they did, we would have soon seen our major cities wiped out in mushroom clouds.

The whole point of this is to expose the Democrats and the media for the treacherous fools they are, and to stop them from leading the country off a cliff to destruction; and to convincingly thrash them in 2004, 2008 and 2012 so America will be safer from terrorism.

Chapter II

✦

Why I Can't Sit on the Fence Anymore and Why I Am Writing This Book

I love America. I love the songs we used to sing in grade school—"My County Tis of Thee", "America the Beautiful", "God Bless America", and of course, our National Anthem, "The Star Spangled Banner." I love the way we can vote, and the way we can read many different newspapers with different viewpoints, and the way we can freely speak our mind without fear of being locked up in jail. I love our court system, imperfect as it is, where we are presumed innocent until proven guilty, and every accused person is able to be tried in front of a jury of their peers.

I love the landscape of America—the beautiful pine forests of the Southeast, the gorgeous mountains of the Rockies, the autumn leaves changing to gold in New England, and the green blue waters off the white sand beaches of Florida.

I love our churches, and our Wal-Marts and Home Depots and beautiful shopping malls, where we can buy the best merchandise from all over the world at the best prices.

I love our space program where we are helping not just Americans but people from all nations to go to the International Space Station, and someday, I know we'll go to Mars. You know, we need to go to Mars, and colonize it, not just for the sake of exploration, not just for the incredible tourist attractions of a Martian Grand Canyon four times deeper than our Grand Canyon and 2600 miles long, and mountains three times taller than Mt. Everest, but because someday our beautiful green earth may explode in nuclear war, and our Martian colony may be the only way to continue the human race. So our space program is essential, not just for the sake of exploration, but perhaps for our very survival.

But I digress—let me get back to America!

I love our sports traditions—football in the fall, baseball and hotdogs and fireworks in the summer, and soccer and tennis and the NBA and all the sports you can think of.

I love our history, most of it. I love our heroes of history—George Washington, Thomas Jefferson, Ben Franklin, Abraham Lincoln, Martin Luther King, and countless others. I love our military heroes that fought and died on the beaches of Normandy so Europe could be free, and so an evil tyrant could not conquer the world, and who fought in countless battles on foreign shores for freedom.

I'll always remember Memorial Day when I was ten years old, proudly marching down the street in the annual Memorial Day Parade our town had, beating the bass drum in my school's marching band. People lined the streets, waving Old Glory, honoring our brave military men and women who gave their all so we could be free.

I love the way America has been forged from so many immigrants from so many countries. I love the way people can come from another country, oppressed by grinding poverty, disease, and political dictatorships, and have a new life in America. With hard work and dedication they can make a good living, and get good health care, and get free education for their kids, and their kids can become lawyers and doctors and anything they want.

The American Dream is real, my friends, and that is why people from all over the globe want to come to America.

The most important thing I love about America is our freedom to worship God as we please. Half of the Pilgrims died in that first cruel winter. They came to America because they wanted to breathe free and worship God as they wished. It was even more important than life itself. And those that survived, thrived. And more and more people came to America, and their noble experiment in liberty became the greatest nation on Earth.

God has indeed blessed America!

However a dark cloud has come over our great nation. We have turned away from God's ways, and we have gotten away from His protection. We have let the leadership of the liberal left take us away from the Promised Land back out into the desert, away from God's protection, and now we have been cruelly struck by Satan and his minions on September 11, 2001; a day that, like Pearl Harbor, will live forever in infamy, but a day which unfortunately will probably be outdone a million times over in the very near future if we do not change our course away from evil, sin, and the weakness of the liberal left Democratic leadership. We have been given a brief reprieve in the narrow election of the courageous George

W. Bush, despite the evil and corrupt attempts of Al Gore and the Democrats to steal the election.

Our lives hang in the balance—if we re-elect George W. Bush in 2004, and a clear majority of Republicans (hopefully over sixty percent in the Senate so we can stop the inherently unconstitutional practice of Senate filibusters by the Democrats), we have a good, fighting chance to survive the incredibly dangerous world that is every day growing worse—a world full of terrorists that want to blow up our cities with nuclear bombs if they can get them, and deluge the U.S. mail with anthrax letters, and fill our subways with sarin—and a world with rogue countries like North Korea and Iran and Syria that would sell or give these weapons to Osama bin Laden and his al-Qaida and other terrorists, or hit our allies and even our own nation with nuclear missiles—missiles built with our own technology that the worst traitor since the Rosenbergs, Bill Clinton, gave to China, who then gave to North Korea! I first heard about this from Duke Cunningham, Congressman from California, (in his younger days Duke was a fighter pilot and was the inspiration for the movie Top Gun) and then I also read about it in Michael Savage's blockbuster book, Savage Nation, and Rich Lowry's masterful book Legacy. Before the great traitor Clinton gave our missile technology to the Chinese (over intense objections from the CIA and FBI), Chinese missiles were falling off the launch pads and exploding. Now since Clinton gave them our technology, China has now improved their missiles and can now hit our cities with nuclear bombs, and the Chinese gave this technology to North Korea, so now the North Koreans can not only hit Seoul if they want to, they can hit San Francisco and Los Angeles and San Diego with nuclear bombs! If this is not treason, I don't know what is. And the reason Clinton gave our missile technology to the Chinese was so the Chinese would give millions of dollars to the 1996 Clinton campaign, which the Clinton campaign had to return when they got caught because it is illegal to accept campaign money from foreign countries, for obvious reasons. So now, thanks to traitor Bill Clinton, North Korea can nuke our troops in South Korea, our friends in Japan and the Philippines, and our own cities on the West Coast!

Bill Clinton sold out our country for a few lousy sordid campaign bucks he ended up having to give back. Although some campaign bucks he got to keep, as Rich Lowry, editor of The National Review, explains in his excellent book Legacy: Paying the Price for the Clinton Years, saying that Clinton got millions of dollars from Silicon Valley satellite companies that he allowed to sell our missile technology to the Chinese.

The Rosenbergs were hanged for their treason of giving U.S. nuclear secrets to the Soviet Union.

Bill Clinton should be tried for treason.

If San Francisco or Los Angeles or San Diego ever gets destroyed in a nuclear mushroom cloud, you can thank Bill Clinton. Getting back to my original theme—I love America. Until September 11 happened, I was content to stay on the sidelines. I didn't like all the things the Democrats were doing, and I voted Republican, but I was content to live my life and do my work as a doctor and help people on an individual basis, and I didn't feel I needed to get involved in politics.

But when September 11 happened, my whole world changed forever, just like everyone's did. No longer can I sit on the sidelines and watch the Democrats screw up and ruin and eventually totally destroy our wonderful, beautiful country. The Democrat screw ups before were upsetting to me—their push to legalize the immoral practice of abortion in 1973 and their determined efforts to continue and maintain this horrible curse on America's back; Jimmy Carter's giving away of the Panama Canal, which our ancestors sweated and died to build, his undermining of the Shah of Iran and the consequent disaster of the rise of the Mullahs and then the Iran Hostage Crisis and his miserable handling of it, and his and the Democrats' bureaucratic over-regulation and stifling of the free market economy which lead to double digit inflation and interest rates (remember interest rates of 22%?)—all of which thankfully lead to the election of Ronald Reagan, which along with George H.W. Bush's presidency got us back on track (if anyone thinks Bill Clinton is responsible for the boom economy of the 90's, they are sadly mistaken—it was the sound policies of Reagan and Bush and the Republican Congress that prepared the fertile ground for the boom—(and it was the grave error of Alan Greenspan who foolishly raised interest rates in the late 90's fearing an inflation that wasn't even coming that stalled the economy—fortunately he realized his mistake and back-tracked and lowered the interest rates, and now the economy is finally coming back (and I admit there were other forces hurting the economy as well, such as the corporate fraud of Enron, WorldCom, and HealthSouth and others, and the foolishness of the dot coms (dot.bombs). But getting back to the screw ups of the Democrats (and the Democratic Congress—Senate and House—not all of them, but a lot of them—are just as responsible as the Democratic Presidents)—there came a Democratic screw up who forever put Jimmy Carter and every bad past president totally in the shade—the disastrous, treasonous, ruinous, wrecker of America, Bill Clinton.

Bill Clinton had <u>numerous chances</u> to get Osama bin Laden, and he refused to take Osama each time, even when Sudan offered Osama "on a silver platter," as Sean Hannity so aptly puts it in his brilliant book <u>Let Freedom Ring</u> (Page 17). Clinton is also responsible for freeing Mohammed Atta from an Israeli prison. Mohammed Atta, the lead hijacker of September 11, was in jail for life in an Israeli prison for killing 42 Israelis in a car bomb attack. However, Clinton pressured Israel to free Atta and many other terrorists as part of a Palestinian peace plan that predictably failed. So, thanks to Bill Clinton, Mohammed Atta was free to lead the attack on the World Trade Center on September 11, 2001.

Bill Clinton's weak and pathetic response to the increasing terror attacks on the U.S. by Osama, al-Qaida, and others (note the title of this book) allowed the travesty of September 11 to happen.

After September 11, I couldn't sit on the sidelines any more. I saw how the weak policies of Jimmy Carter and Bill Clinton and John Kerry and the Democrats had weakened our national security to the point where not only did September 11 happen, but much worse things can and probably will happen to our once-safe country.

In 1994, when it became clear that North Korea was actively violating the Nuclear Non-proliferation Treaty and was in the process of building a nuclear weapon, Clinton sent Jimmy Carter, "who could out-appease even Bill Clinton," (according to Rich Lowry, editor of <u>The National Review</u>, in <u>Legacy: Paying the Price for the Clinton Years</u> on page 239) to North Korea to solve the crisis. Jimmy and Bill came up with a typically weak appeasement plan, the Framework Agreement, which did not stop North Korea from building nukes but which only glossed over the problem and gave the false appearance of a solution which bought more time for the North Koreans to develop their nuclear bombs, of which they now have at least six and are actively making more.

Carter and Clinton gave millions of dollars of food and energy aid to North Korea, plus <u>helped</u> build light-water nuclear reactors which can provide fuel for nuclear weapons, in return for North Korea's promise that it would stop trying to build nuclear weapons. Carter and Clinton, foolishly trusting the North Korean's promise, despite the CIA predicting North Korea would cheat, happily thought they had "solved the problem".[1]

Famous last words! Now the North Koreans have nuclear weapons, and, thanks to Bill Clinton, the missile technology to deliver them, and, most frightening of all, the North Koreans, famous (or infamous, I suppose, is the better

---

1.   <u>Legacy</u>, by Rich Lowry, page 238, originally attributed to Gertz, page 123.

word) for selling weapons to anyone anytime anywhere, can now sell a nuclear weapon to an al-Qaida terrorist! Look out, New York City!

Who will ever forget the twin Towers toppling down into billowing clouds of smoke?

Who will ever forget the thousands of innocent victims, including the heroic firemen and policemen of New York?

When I was a kid we lived in New Jersey and my dad commuted by train every day to Manhattan. My dad called one of his old friends in New Jersey after the September 11 attack, and his friend gave him the news that 70 people in our old county died—70 moms and dads, leaving kids without one parent. And county after county, and indeed country after country, had similar numbers of dead.

And this is just the beginning. If we don't stop the terrorists and the rogue nations that are supporting them and the rogue nations that are developing or already have nuclear and biological and chemical weapons, we are going to see carnage and bloodshed and disaster in America like we have never seen before, and which we may not even survive.

Instead of seeing the horrible picture of the World Trade Centers imploding, with three thousand victims, we will see all of Manhattan and Washington, D.C. going up in mushroom clouds, with millions of victims. We will see hundreds of anthrax letters (if a letter could brush up against an anthrax letter in a post office and kill a grandmother in Connecticut, think what would happen if the terrorists put pin pricks in each letter they sent to let the anthrax spores cross-contaminate thousands of letters) and we will see thousands of our elderly die horrible deaths from anthrax pneumonia.

And we will see sarin kill thousands of commuters on our subways. And much, much, worse. We may see our cities on the West Coast go up in mushroom clouds by nuclear attacks from North Korea (thank you, Bill Clinton). And worse. And worse. And worse.

So I can't sit on the sidelines anymore and watch the Democrats screw up America, this time fatally. I can't sit by and watch their liberal left weakness ruin the security of America. I can't sit by and watch them bow down to the wimps of the European Union and the United Nations, and let them tie our hands so we can't kill the terrorists and stop the rogue nations who support them.

So I'm jumping in the battle. I'm getting involved in politics. And I'm writing this book.

Which brings me to the title—Saddam's Attacks on America—1993; September 11, 2001; and the Anthrax Attacks! The reason I am writing this is to show that Saddam Hussein clearly was behind the bombing of the World Trade Center in 1993, the destruction of the World Trade Center on September 11, 2001 (he finally succeeded in his goal with the help of his hit-man, Osama bin Laden), and the attack on the Pentagon, and the attack of the anthrax letters through the U.S. mail in October of 2001.

The reason I am showing Saddam was behind all these attacks on America is to show that America's war on Iraq was <u>absolutely necessary</u> to prevent further and worse (nuclear) attacks on America, especially since Saddam was only months away from getting nuclear weapons and either giving them to terrorists or using them along with his 400 mile range al-Hussein missiles (he had at least eight of them—I saw them in a photograph taken by British Intelligence on the front page of the <u>Birmingham</u> (Alabama) <u>News</u>—why didn't the rest of the media pick up on this? Media bias, perhaps? Probably!) And using nuclear threat to carry out his eventual plan to conquer Kuwait and Saudi Arabia and the whole Persian Gulf—Saddam's ultimate goal as the new "Saladin."

If we had waited a few more months it would have been too late—Saddam would have had nukes and he could nuke Tel Aviv or our troops or Riyadh or even Greece or Turkey with his 400-mile range al-Hussein missiles—forget the al-Samood missiles with their 93-mile range that the inept U.N. inspectors were focusing on. Saddam was actively seeking nuclear weapons, and he would have eventually made them or bought them from North Korea or Pakistan, and then "Look out, World!"

So the War on Iraq was <u>absolutely necessary</u> for the security of America and to prevent a third World War—this time a devastating <u>nuclear</u> World War, in the Middle East. The War on Iraq has stopped the immediate threat of Saddam giving nukes to terrorists to blow up Manhattan and Washington D.C., and for the time being stopped the threat of anthrax letters, although it appears he sent biological weapons mobile labs in trailer trucks to Syria and we probably will have to go into Syria and destroy them since Syria sponsors <u>many</u> terrorist groups in Syria and in the Bekka Valley of Lebanon. Which brings me to the point of my book—I love America, and I hate to see it destroyed by the sickening, pathetic, self-serving demagogues of the liberal left Democratic leadership, and I mean specifically the sorry losers that are presently running for the Democratic presidential nomination, plus Ted Kennedy and Tom Daschle.

Each one of these arrogant misleaders, with the lone exception of Joe Lieberman, has the absolute gall to bash President Bush for taking over Iraq and eliminating the imminent threat to the U.S. of Saddam Hussein. Here is the liberal left, who <u>caused</u> the security problems in the first place, which allowed America to be attacked by terrorists, now <u>blaming</u> the <u>solver</u> of the problem, George W. Bush!

They blame him because they say, "we haven't found weapons of mass destruction." Well folks, every major nation's intelligence agencies have told us for years, "Saddam <u>does</u> (or did) have weapons of mass destruction"!

We all <u>know</u> he did!

He had months before the war started, thanks to the dilly-dallying of the United Nations, to hide his weapons, destroy them, or ship them to Syria (before the war started, Israeli intelligence showed Saddam was <u>sending convoys of trailer trucks</u> [containing mobile biological and chemical weapons labs] to Syria).

We have already found two such mobile biological weapons labs buried in Iraq—they are identical to the mobile labs Colin Powell showed the United Nations prior to the war. They had been scrubbed clean with cleanser to eliminate any traces of anthrax or other agents but the fact remains they could easily be cranked up to produce enough toxins to kill hundreds of thousands of people. And we will find more. The suggestion that the buried mobile labs were merely intended to produce hydrogen is ludicrous. Why do you have to bury a mobile lab if it is only an innocent hydrogen producer? Saddam buried his mobile biological and chemical weapons labs for the same reason he buried some of his fighter planes—so he could use them later! As Congressman Terry Everett so aptly puts it "Subsequent U.S. inspections of Iraq already show evidence of hidden biological weapons labs, Iraqi efforts to destroy evidence of their weapons of mass destruction program, and plans to purchase banned missiles from North Korea."

Remember the 3,000 chemical protection suits we found the Iraqis had when we entered Iraq? Why would the Iraqi army have chemical weapons suits? Because they were considering using chemical weapons on us! The reason they did <u>not</u> use the chemical weapons on us is because they realized they were going to be defeated so Saddam had them destroy, hide, and/or send to Syria all the chemical and biological weapons he had!

Why did Saddam endure crippling U.N. sanctions to keep U.N. Inspectors from fully examining his country, and even go to war? Because he was making chemical and biological weapons and seeking materials to make nuclear weapons, and he did not want to stop his weapons of mass destruction programs for anything.

It is wonderful that we have captured Saddam Hussein. However, we still need to stop all the Iraqi terrorists and the terrorists that Iran and al-Qaida are sending into Iraq. When we finally fully stabilize Iraq, and kill or imprison all the

Baathist and Fedayeen and al-Qaida thugs and Iran terrorists that are plaguing Iraq, and finally achieve a safe and secure Iraq, many Iraqi scientists will no longer fear the terrorists, and they will come forward with proof of Saddam's chemical, biological, <u>and nuclear</u> programs.

Already an Iraqi scientist has confessed to having a centrifuge in his home that is for the purpose of refining uranium and although he says it was from 1991 I suspect he hid it very recently, like just before the War on Iraq.

Similarly, another Iraqi scientist was found to have a botulin sample in his refrigerator. Although he says it was a sample from 1991, it is much more likely that it is a recent sample from just before the War on Iraq, when Saddam probably ordered his scientists to hide biological, chemical and nuclear weapons program components in their homes and elsewhere, so when the war was over they could quickly re-constitute those programs.

One of Saddam's Ministers, whom we have in custody, has recently admitted that Iraq was importing illegal goods into the country—why? For their weapons programs! The Iraqi scientists are afraid to tell us anything now because of the terrorists in Iraq that threaten their very lives and the lives of our soldiers, but when we finally stomp out the last of these terrorists like cockroaches, and Iraq becomes truly safe, the Iraqi scientists will finally open up and tell us about Saddam's weapons of mass destruction programs.

And the sorry Democrat losers running for President will have to admit they were dead wrong. The liberal left Democratic leadership is our nation's worst enemy. I hope when the election comes in November 2004 we will <u>bury</u> these wimpy Democrats who couldn't beat their way out of a wet paper bag and couldn't defend our country at all, in a huge election landslide that will give them the thrashing they deserve and that will re-elect George W. Bush so America can be safe. How can America even consider electing the weak-on-defense wishy-washy flip-flopper John Kerry? He voted <u>time after time</u> to cut our defense and intelligence budgets, and even voted just two weeks after September 11 to cut our intelligence budget! How intelligent was that?! Electing the weak-on-defense John Kerry would be a disaster for America and the World. He would certainly pull us out of Iraq, and then al-Qaida and the terrorists would take over Iraq and use the 10 billion dollars of annual oil revenue to fund their world-wide terror attacks. And we would lose the War on Terror. And we will lose our cities in nuclear attacks by terrorists. But if we re-elect the courageous, man of action George W. Bush, we have a chance to win the War on Terror and protect America.

God bless America! And America bless God! If we honor God and re-elect a Christian President, and our nation turns back to God, God will again protect America and bless us once more.

Chapter III

◆

Saddam's Attacks

Saddam Hussein was <u>very</u> angry when America forced him out of Kuwait in the 1991 Gulf War. It was a good thing George H.W. Bush persevered and went to war, over the objections of most of the sorry Democrats who are total gutless wonders and who have no concept of what it takes to defend our nation's and the free world's security on a global scale. If George Bush '41 had not gone to war, if the cowardly Democrats had succeeded in voting him down, all hell would have broken loose in the Middle East. Saddam, after consolidating his conquest of Kuwait, would have then invaded Saudi Arabia, which would have folded like a deck of cards. The Saudi Arabian army would have been nothing more than a speed bump in the road to Saddam's conquest. Then he would have 50% of the world's oil reserves.

People who foolishly chant in protest about, "No blood for oil" and who say we should not go to war for oil are very naïve. Oil is the lifeblood of the <u>whole world's economy</u>. Someday hopefully we can use hydrogen power and no longer depend so much on the Middle East for oil. But until that day comes we must be realistic about the need to protect ours and the rest of the world's oil reserves in the Middle East. Without that oil we would have a global economic depression that would make the 1929 depression look like a picnic. And we are not trying to get the oil fields for us, the U.S.; we simply want to keep the oil in the control of the countries that own it instead of unstable rogue nations. We never took the oil fields of Kuwait—we <u>returned</u> control <u>to Kuwait</u> after Saddam had stolen them.

And the "blood for oil" protesters overlook the main reason for stopping Saddam, which is far greater than oil. Once Saddam conquered Kuwait and then Saudi Arabia, he would aim for the whole Persian Gulf. And here is the most chilling thing to remember—although our intelligence sources thought Saddam was at least a year away from developing nuclear weapons at the time of the Gulf War, it was found after the war that he was only <u>six months away</u> from having nuclear weapons! Saddam is known to say that his only mistake in invading Kuwait was that he should have waited just a few more months when he would have had nuclear weapons.

Saddam is exactly like Adolph Hitler in that he has a power-mad craving to control the world. Like a malignant cancer, he would have just kept growing further, taking over more and more countries. He would have taken over much of the Persian Gulf if George Bush hadn't stopped him, and when finally the Europeans would start to whine and beg the U.S. to stop Saddam as he threatened Greece and Turkey and Europe, we would have found Saddam with hundreds of nukes, with all the major cities of Europe targeted with long range nuclear missiles.

Saddam, being the crafty but insane gambler that he is, just like Hitler, had no fear of MAD (Mutually Assured Destruction). Some naïve people like Chris Matthews on "Softball" argued vociferously that Saddam would never nuke Israel because Israel would then nuke Baghdad. But Chris Matthews failed to discern the true nature of Saddam—he was so madly insane—clever, cunning, crafty, but insane in his military planning (remember his irrational statement at the beginning of the Gulf War, that Iraq would win the "Mother of all Battles" even though the U.S. and Coalition forces clearly had overwhelming superiority?) The Soviets were at least logical and MAD deterred them from blowing up our cities because they were rational and did not want their cities blown up. But we know that Saddam is so reckless that he doesn't care if Baghdad gets blown up—he had 50 miles of underground tunnels and bunkers (built by the Germans, thank you very much to our "allies" the Germans). We know Saddam didn't care about his people—as long as he was safe in his bunker, who cares if Baghdad gets blown up?

Saddam was truly an incredibly poor military planner—a military goof ball. Instead of a Saladin, he was a Gomer Pyle. Look at his idiotic attempt to go against the Coalition forces in the Gulf War—he had his army spread out in the desert where they were sitting ducks for our Air Force and were decimated. It was sheer madness to even go against the Coalition forces. His air force fled to Iran. His army was a joke. His soldiers surrendered to Italian photojournalists on one occasion! So much for the "Mother of all Battles"! And look at Saddam's total miscalculation and lack of military skill in the Iraq war. He should have given up and never even tried to face our military superiority. But since he was foolish enough to try, he should have at least mounted some kind of defense. Instead, he did nothing but burn some tires around Baghdad. Not one Iraqi air force plane even dared to get off the ground. Not one bridge was blown when the Coalition trekked from Basra to Baghdad. As a military planner, Saddam was a pathetic failure, as even one of his own Ministers now admits.

About the only response the Iraqis had were the suicidal attacks of the Fedayeen against Coalition Forces, unless you count the ridiculous plan to send "suicide bombers" in a convoy of 1500 SUV's to attack us—it was a suicidal mission all right as soon as our air force got a bead on them.

All this is to point out the irrationality of Saddam, whose rogue nature made the policy of "Mutually Assured Destruction" not work with him.

Saddam, for all his military ineptness, would have been a real danger in just a few months if he had obtained nuclear weapons. This would have made even a military klutz into one dangerous dude. As it was pointed out before, in the introductory chapter, Saddam was very close to getting nukes, which will be proved soon when we get the Iraqi scientists to talk, and since he already had at least eight al-Hussein missiles with 400 mile range, he could have easily threatened to nuke Tel Aviv or Riyadh or even Turkey or Greece, and then moved into Kuwait. Chris Matthews will soon be proved, when all the evidence of WMD (Weapons of Mass Destruction) comes in, and we see how close Saddam was to having nukes, to have made one of the stupidest statements of all time—"smoking is more dangerous than Saddam Hussein." Would smoking ruins of Tel Aviv and Riyadh, and when Saddam gave nukes to al-Qaida, smoking ruins of Washington D.C. and Manhattan be enough to convince Chris that Saddam was dangerous? Not to mention Saddam's VX nerve gas and anthrax mobile labs (we have two of them in custody—they were scrubbed clean because the Iraqis knew they were going to lose the war and they knew they'd better get rid of their chemical and biological weapons). And when I demonstrate in just a bit that it was Saddam who initiated the anthrax attacks through Mohammed Atta and his roommate in Boca Raton, Florida and his fellow hijackers and their roommates in Trenton, New Jersey, it will become even more clear what an imminent and absolute threat that Saddam was to the people of America. Here's a thought—it is said that there was a plane with hijackers in England on September 11 that was supposed to crash into Parliament but because all planes were grounded worldwide after the first planes hit the World Trade Towers, that plane was grounded, and the hijackers were foiled, but got away.

Thank God that plane didn't hit Parliament. But if it had, don't you think the English people would have been more supportive to Tony Blair's courageous move to remove Saddam? If German and France and Russia had been hit on September 11, by al-Qaida terrorists under Osama bin Laden instigated by Saddam

Hussein, I think they would have been more supportive of our efforts to remove Saddam.

I will demonstrate soon the clear-cut link between Saddam and Osama and the hijackers and September 11, and the anthrax attacks, but first let me get back to the point, in the first sentence of this chapter, that Saddam Hussein was very angry at the United States for blocking his goal of obtaining Kuwait. He was more than angry. His anger was the seething, satanic rage of a Hitlerian madman who liked to torture people to death and then watch the videos so he could enjoy their suffering over and over. This was perhaps one of the greatest seething anger and hate that has ever existed in history, a seething anger and hate that tried to topple the World Trade Center through his hit-man Osama bin Laden in 1993, and which finally succeeded and manifested its hideous expression in the horrible deaths of three thousand people, and the deaths of the people killed by the crash into the Pentagon, and the people killed in the crash of the plane that went down in Pennsylvania because the heroic passengers (we will never forget the immortal words of Todd Beamer—"Let's Roll") fought the terrorists and crashed the plane that the hijackers had meant for the U.S. Capitol.

Saddam hated the U.S. with all the twisted evil his horrible mind could muster, and to get revenge, he attacked the U.S. in the bombing of the World Trade Center in 1993; the destruction of the World Trade Center and the attack on the Pentagon, and the attempted attack on the Capitol on September 11, 2001; and in the anthrax attacks of October 2001, all through his hit-man, Osama bin Laden and his al-Qaida operatives—Ramzi Yousef and his accomplices in 1993, and Mohammed Atta and his gang, (and their roommates who sent the anthrax letters from Boca Raton, Florida and Trenton, New Jersey) in 2001.

So the Iraq war was payback to Saddam and also so Saddam would not hurt us again only much much worse. I'll never forget the U.S. tank with the words "PAYBACK" written on its gun barrel!

Some talking heads like Chris Matthews (I know I have been picking on him, but his biased and slanted anti-war views were so egregious I just have to point them out) went on and on saying "Isn't it just incredible that the American people think that Saddam had something to do with September 11?"

You know why the American people think that, Chris? Because they have common sense, unlike the talking airheads on some shows. Wake up and smell the coffee, Chris! Saddam hated the United States and he got back at the United States by using Osama bin Laden to destroy the World Trade Center and to send the anthrax letters. And he would have done much worse to us if President Bush hadn't had the courage to stop him, despite all you and other media folk and a lot of Democrats in Congress did to try to stop President Bush from taking out the Hitler of the 21st century. And herein lies the greatness of George W. Bush, who had the guts, the courage and the insight, helped by some of his advisors and the equally courageous Tony Blair, to stop this modern day Hitler <u>before</u> he could kill 50 million people, or more, like the first Hitler did.

When Hitler marched his 200,000 troops in the Rhineland in clear violation of the Armistice treaty in the years just before World War II, there were 1 <u>million</u> two hundred thousand French troops just across the Rhine that could have and should have wiped him out. However the French leadership showed their usual spineless cowardice and failed to act at the time when Hitler's army and power were small and he had not yet grown into the "Blitzkrieg Behometh" that took World War II and 50 million deaths to stop. If only the French had had the guts to do a "preemptive" strike on Hitler at the time of Hitler's illegal provocation in the Rhineland, millions of people would not have had to die later in World War II.

So how <u>dare</u> the Democrats criticize George W. Bush for wisely and courageously taking out Saddam before he got nukes and could give them to al-Qaida to blow up our cities or use them to take over the whole Persian Gulf! The Democrats, in addition to being fools, are arrogant and obnoxious fools who have the colossal <u>nerve</u> to bash President Bush for saving America and the rest of the world from the madman Saddam Hussein!

And General Wesley Clark, the latest addition to the Democratic Presidential Follies, especially should be ashamed of his tactical ignorance and colossal arrogance in criticizing President Bush for taking out Saddam. As a military man he should know the huge tactical importance of taking out Saddam before he got nuclear weapons. But General Clark has a backward way of looking at things, as is clearly evident by his chummy friendship with the Serb general Ratko Mladic. Even after Ratko (what an apt name!) slaughtered thousands of Bosnians in Srebrenika, and was being sought as a war criminal, Wesley Clark was drinking wine with him and even traded military hats with him! Wesley Clark is no Eisenhower; indeed, he is more along the lines of General George McClellan in the Civil War who ran against Lincoln in the Presidential election of 1864 with giving in to the Confederacy as his main platform. Hopefully Wesley Clark, or "General Flip-Flop" as I like to call him due to his frequent about-faces on issues, will, like McClellan before him, fade into the obscurity of defeat, as will the greatest Flip-Flopper of them all, the human waffle, Hanoi John Kerry. Even some of Kerry's comrades in Vietnam said he was a poor commander, and they couldn't stand him and said he is not fit to be President (See the Swift Boats Society website).

Kerry admitted that he himself had committed, in Viet Nam, atrocities worse than were committed recently at Abu Ghraib prison in Iraq. My opinion is that a person, who would commit atrocities like that, even during the pressures of war, is not fit to be President of the United States. Furthermore, John Kerry, like Jane Fonda, communicated with North Vietnamese authorities during war time, which is illegal under U.S. law.

Grant Hibbard, the commander to whom John Kerry reported one of his injuries on December 3, 1968, wrote in a letter to the editor published in a June 2004 edition of USA Today that Kerry had wounded himself with a M-79 grenade round he fired too close. There was no hostile fire from the enemy that night. Kerry wanted a Purple Heart, and Commander Hibbard refused, because a Purple Heart must be received in action with an enemy. The wound was a scratch of shrapnel one centimeter in length and two millimeters in diameter.

Hibbard goes on to say, "Kerry orchestrated his way out of Vietnam and then testified, under oath, before Congress that we, his comrades had committed horrible war crimes. This testimony was a lie and slandered honorable men. We, who actually were there, believe he is unfit to command our sons and daughters."

And, just as John Kerry is unfit to be our Commander-in-Chief, his boyish running mate, John Edwards, is in no way fit to be Vice President, just a heart beat away from the Presidency.

John Edwards has no foreign policy experience whatsoever, and indeed has little political experience. He has a happy beaming face and a cheerful disposition, but when you look closer at him you see he is an empty shell of hot air. He voted against funding our troops in Iraq. He refused to take a stand on the horror of partial birth abortion and abstained from voting both times Congress voted to ban it. In several multi-million dollar court cases Edwards used "junk science" to convince juries that doctors were responsible for cerebral palsy birth defects, when real science disproves this. He talks about rich America and poor America, but he actually hurt the middle class by ripping off the system to enrich himself by 40 million dollars as a personal injury trial lawyer, thus increasing the costs to everyone of medical costs and costs passed on to consumers, and he helped aggravate the national problem of doctors and hospitals having to shut down in some areas due to lawsuits and increased liability insurance costs. Speaker of the House, Dennis Hastert, says that lawsuits have added 20% to the cost of American products, which hurts us in competing with the rest of the world.

And he and Kerry have voted against tax cuts, and indeed all their wonderful-sounding plans involve more taxes for everyone, including the middle class, who are already paying about 50% of their income in taxes of all types (Federal, state,

FICA, gasoline taxes, etc.) And now we find that Edwards avoided half a million dollars in taxes to Medicare by using a very questionable tax avoidance scheme by making himself a corporation. In other words, he wants you, the tax payer, to pay higher Medicare taxes while he, the slick multi-millionaire, cheats and avoids paying his Medicare tax. And even though Kerry and Edwards talk about fighting terror, all their talk is a bunch of hot air. John Edwards was behind in preliminary polls to regain his Senate seat in North Carolina because he is too liberal. Do we really want two lawyers, who are ranked the most liberal Senator (Kerry) and the fourth most liberal Senator (Edwards) in the U.S. Senate, both to the left of Hilary Clinton and Ted Kennedy, to be our leaders?

An ounce of prevention is worth a pound of cure. George W. Bush is one of the greatest U.S. presidents ever, because he had the insight and courage, even though much of the world opposed him, to preemptively take out the immense threat of Saddam Hussein before Saddam could get nukes. Bush and Blair took out Saddam before he could start nuclear World War III, and President Bush and Blair saved probably 50 million or more lives. Imagine if Saddam got nuclear weapons, then took over Kuwait and Saudi Arabia, threatening to destroy Tel Aviv and Riyadh if anyone opposed him. If weak wimpy Democrats happened to be in power, they would dither around and ask the United Nations to solve the problem, which is like asking Caspar Milquetoast to stop the neighborhood bully (remember the wimpy U.N. "security" forces watching helplessly as thousands of unarmed Bosnian civilians were massacred by the Serbs in the U.N. "Safe" areas in Kosovo?) and remember Somalia? The reason U.S. troops got killed was because they were put under U.N. command which totally screwed up the whole situation. So asking the U.N. to solve the problem of Saddam Hussein is like asking Tinker Bell to come sprinkle us all with fairy dust so that the bad terrorists won't hurt us anymore.

And you know what? Whatever has happened to the guts of America? In Teddy Roosevelt's day if 18 U.S. soldiers were killed in Somalia or Tripoli or anywhere, and their bodies dragged through the street, I assure you Teddy Roosevelt himself would have led the U.S. Marines to totally destroy those Somali warlords who dared to kill and desecrate American soldiers.

Teddy Roosevelt would have led a massive retaliatory force and crushed those pathetic Somali warlords and taught them and the world a lesson. But what did we do? We left in retreat.

What did we do when Lebanon-based terrorists from Hamas destroyed our Marine base in Lebanon in 1983? Did we go in with a retaliatory force and obliterate them? No, we left in retreat.

And you know what makes me furious about that situation? I learned on Fox TV several months ago that our CIA had the terrorists who were planning to destroy our Marine base in their sights, and wanted to take them out, knew they were planning some terrorist operation, but the diplomatic bureaucrats (bumble-crats) wouldn't let them because it wasn't U.S. policy to assassinate terrorists. So the terrorists assassinated 241 of our marines.

Well let me tell you something—it better become U.S. policy to assassinate any terrorist or rogue world leader that is planning to harm the U.S. We need to kill them before they kill us.

Preemptive strikes are the way to stop terrorists. If someone were about to kill you, wouldn't you like to kill him first?

Preemptive strikes are the way to protect Americans from future (and worse) September 11's.

So Thank God Bush and Blair did a preemptive strike on Saddam Hussein (although in actual fact, since Saddam attacked America first, in 1993, September 11, 2001 and in the anthrax attacks, technically the war on Iraq was in response to Saddam's attacks on America and thus was not truly a preemptive attack). Thank God Bush and Blair did not let the cowardly and self-serving nations of France and Germany and Russia and China and the U.N. stop us from taking out Saddam before he got nukes (and, as history will soon show, he was very close to getting nukes).

As we have mentioned before, if only the cowardly French leadership had pre-emptively taken out Adolf Hitler when he marched 200,000 German troops in 1939 in the Rhineland, in clear violation of the armistice of World War I. One million two hundred thousand French troops were on the other side of the river, and could have easily crushed Hitler, and would have been perfectly legal in doing so since Hitler was breaking the Treaty of Versailles. If the French had any guts at all they could have and should have stopped Hitler right then, before he grew in power and the French had to call on America to help them. Had the French had the courage then that George W. Bush and Tony Blair have now, they could have easily stopped Hitler and prevented him from killing 50 million people in World War II.

So for the French to criticize George Bush and Tony Blair for doing the right thing is the worst hypocrisy and the most cowardly and self-serving political move ever made by the once great, now pathetic nation of France. France and Russia and Germany didn't want to stop Saddam Hussein because of their rich oil contracts. For a few lousy dollars they sold out the security of the free world.

And now we find that the French and Russians were getting <u>huge</u> amounts of money from Iraq illegally from the U.N. Oil for Food scam.

It was the French who built the Osirik nuclear reactor for Saddam that the Israelis thankfully destroyed in 1981 (the Israelis were condemned for their preemptive action, even by the U.S., but now it looks like one of the best military decisions ever made!)

It was the Germans who built the 50 miles of underground bunkers and tunnels that Saddam planned to hide in if he ever nuked Tel Aviv and the Israelis nuked him back—he didn't care about his people dying in Baghdad in a nuclear war, as long as he was safe in his German-built bunkers.

It was the Russians who a few weeks before the Iraq War gave Saddam a worldwide list of assassins for hire, in case Saddam wanted to bump anyone off (like President Bush, for example?)

So let me tell you something, folks. We don't owe the French or the Russians or the Germans anything except a kick in the rear. And we owe a kick in the rear to the Noble Prize Committee that gave Jimmy Carter the peace prize as an underhanded way to give President Bush "a kick in the leg". And we certainly don't owe the joke called the United Nations anything. How can such a group of nations be taken seriously when they had Syria and Libya on the Commission on Human Rights in 2003, and this year are planning to have <u>Cuba</u> be the <u>chairman</u> of the Commission on Human Rights! And they wanted to put the U.S. <u>off</u> the Commission of Human Rights! The U.N. is a disjointed group of nations most of which are dictatorships who have an anti-American and anti-Israeli bias. The U.N.'s total incompetence in Bosnia, where U.N. troops allowed the horrible slaughter of thousands of Bosnians is all the proof we need to never again let the U.N. be in charge of safe-guarding our or anyone's security.

Those who criticize President Bush for going to war "unilaterally" are wrong. He tried to get the U.N. to enforce its own resolutions but when the U.N. refused, he had to defend America's security without the U.N. He did get a Coalition of 30 countries which had the courage to help us!

The United Nations is useful only as a debating society and for humanitarian relief efforts, <u>if that</u>. (There is some evidence that the U.N. is not even a very effective relief organization, and that private groups could do the job a lot better.) In fact, now we know that the U.N. fraudulently used the Oil for Food program in Iraq to embezzle millions of dollars to France, Russia, and even Kofi Annan's son. No wonder the U.N. and France and Russia didn't want Saddam removed from power—it would destroy their graft!

So Bush and Blair did what the French and English could not do in World War II, which was to stop their Hitler (Saddam) preemptively, before he could grow in power, get nukes and kill millions in a nuclear World War III. So let us now praise those two famous men, George W. Bush and Tony Blair. And may their detractors, the Democratic presidential losers, the liberal press, and the EU and the United Nations, be forever shamed that they opposed the most important military action of the new millennium, the war to stop the new Hitler, Saddam Hussein. These detractors, these losers, will forever be, as Sean Hannity so aptly puts it, "On the wrong side of history." And now let us demonstrate the proof that our title proclaims—that Saddam, in his intense hatred for America since we kicked him out of Kuwait in the 1991 Gulf War, instigated and used his hit man Osama bin Laden and al-Qaida to bomb the World Trade Center in 1993, destroy it on September 11, 2001, and send the anthrax letters in October 2001.

There is a great deal of evidence that shows that Saddam was involved in helping Osama bomb the World Trade Center in 1993. Congressman Terry Everett states, "As a senior member of the House Armed Services and Intelligence Committees, and as someone who has personally traveled in Iraq, I can tell you that Saddam's regime did pose a growing threat to America. Its leaders were involved in the planning of the 1993 World Trade Center attacks, were allowing top al-Qaida like Abu Musab al-Zarqawi to operate chemical weapons factories and terrorist cells in Iraq, and were secretly working to create lethal weapons in direct violation of the United Nations' resolutions."

Michael Ledeen, in his landmark book The War Against the Terror Masters, on page 137, writes "Clinton didn't even want to act against a different terror master, one who had tried to murder an American ex-President, who had used weapons of mass destruction against his own people, and who had been involved in the World Trade Center bombing of 1993: Saddam Hussein."

In the June 28, 2004 issue of The Weekly Standard editor William Kristol writes, "The man who mixed the chemicals for the 1993 World Trade Center bomb, Abdul Rahman Yakin, came from and returned to Baghdad, where he lived for the next 10 years."

Ramzi Yousef, the lead bomber, got help from Iraq to get a passport to get him into America to bomb the World Trade Center. And four of his helpers, now in custody, are Iraqis. Certainly Saddam had the motive for his crime of helping Osama bomb the World Trade Center—he hated America and wanted revenge on America for kicking him out of Kuwait in the Gulf War of 1991. And now we turn to September 11, 2001. Saddam Hussein is very, very persistent and determined. His effort in 1993 killed six people and injured more than one thousand, but failed to topple the two spires of the World Trade Center into each other. So he tried again, this time successfully on September 11, 2001.

I saw on Fox TV in autumn of 2002 an Iraqi general who had recently defected to the U.S. say that the 19 hijackers of September 11, 2001 trained on the Boeing 707 that Saddam had just south of Baghdad in the Salman Pak terrorist training camp. The hijackers trained on that Boeing 707, which was for the purpose of training terrorists, just six months before they did the real thing on September 11. Our aerial surveillance photos showed that Boeing 707, out in the desert, away from any airport so it could be secretly used to train hijackers, and when our troops took over Iraq they bombed it and only its charred hulk remains!

Several captured al-Qaida terrorists in custody in Guantanamo have said they trained in Iraq. A terrorist training camp was destroyed in northern Iraq by our troops in the war. Many foreign al-Qaida fought our troops in Iraq, and continue to fight our troops in Afghanistan and Iraq this very day.

Here is more proof of Saddam's leadership role in instigating Osama bin Laden to attack the U.S. on September 11, so Saddam could get revenge on the U.S. for thwarting his conquest of Kuwait. I saw on Fox News one of Saddam's mistresses, who had been his mistress for many years, and who had recently defected to the West, say that she saw Saddam meet with Osama bin Laden several times prior to September 11, and each time Saddam gave Osama a lot of money.

Michael Ledeen in The War Against the Terror Masters on page 179 writes, "The most famous contact between Iraq and Al Qaeda came in Prague, on April 8, 2001, when Mohammed Atta—the key September 11 operative—met with an Iraqi intelligence case officer named al-Ani." "Less than two weeks later he opened an account at the Sun Bank in Florida and $100,000 was transferred into that account from an unknown money-changer in the Persian Gulf. That money probably funded at least part of the September 11 operation."

So we see that Saddam trained the 19 hijackers on his terrorist training Boeing 707 in his terrorist training camp at Salman Pak in the months just before September 11, and he met with Osama bin Laden and gave him large sums of money in the months just before September 11, and he probably gave $100,000 to lead hijacker Mohammed Atta.

Just recently English Intelligence has said that Abu Nidal, the famous terrorist that found sanctuary in Iraq, personally trained the lead hijacker, Mohammed Atta, in Baghdad in the months before September 11. And then Saddam had

Abu Nidal killed so he wouldn't talk, and claimed that Nidal's death was a suicide.

Also the highly regarded Washington paper, The Weekly Standard, in the November 24, 2003 issue published an article titled "Case Closed" in which a top-secret Pentagon report to the Senate Intelligence Committee claimed that Iraq had long-standing ties to the al-Qaida terrorist network and possibly to the September 11 attacks on New York and Washington. I highly recommend reading the full six page article.

Stephen Hayes, the author of the article, writes, "Osama bin Laden and Saddam Hussein had an operational relationship from the early 1990s to 2003 that involved training in explosives and weapons of mass destruction, logistical support for terrorist attacks, al Qaeda training camps and safe haven in Iraq, and Iraqi financial support for al Qaeda—perhaps even for Mohammed Atta—according to a top secret U.S. government memorandum obtained by The Weekly Standard."

The Weekly Standard concludes, "The picture that emerges is one of a history of collaboration between two of America's most determined and dangerous enemies."

It is clear that Saddam Hussein instigated and used Osama bin Laden and his al-Qaida to attack America on September 11.

And a poet in Iraq praised Saddam after September 11 at a large gathering of Saddam and his toadies saying, "The World thinks it was Osama, but it was you, O Great Saddam, who destroyed the World Trade Center."

Next we will demonstrate how Saddam Hussein attacked America using anthrax letters sent by Osama bin Laden's al-Qaida operatives here in the U.S.

The National Enquirer did an excellent article proving this. For those who disparage The National Enquirer, I would say that many of their articles, especially this one, are thoroughly researched, often more so than the mainstream media. Often the Enquirer breaks a story that the mainstream media finally catches and prints a month later. If only our mainstream media, with its huge liberal bias, had not stuck its head in the sand and ignored the obvious Saddam—anthrax link that the Enquirer showed? If only our hapless FBI would follow up on the research done by the Enquirer, they would see where the anthrax came from (Saddam) and quit trying to look like they are accomplishing something by ruining the life and career of Dr. Steven Hatfield, a counter-terrorist expert, who has dedicated his life to fighting terrorism, making him a suspect when it is so obvious that Saddam did it! This reminds me of when the media and the FBI jumped all over Richard Jewell, the security guard who saved peoples' lives at the Olympics in Atlanta by getting them away from the backpack, as his supervisor had instructed him to do. The FBI tried to pin the blame on him, so they could say they "solved" the case, when the whole time it was Eric Rudolph who planted the bomb and Richard Jewell was totally innocent.

I think they ought to fire the guy in charge of the FBI, Mueller, or move him out to pasture, so to speak, and instead put the Arizona FBI agents like Colleen Rowley, who tried to warn us about terrorists using airplanes as weapons, in charge of the FBI. Let's put the active people on top, and retire the deadwood (not just Mueller but the bureaucrats just beneath him who squelched the good FBI agents who were warning us about the terrorists).

And George Tenet has got to go from the CIA. The CIA and the FBI let our country down in letting September 11 happen, as did even more so Clinton and Gore. When agencies screw up that bad, new leadership is needed. Senator Richard Shelby wants George Tenet out, and new and better leadership in, and President Bush should do that.[1] And President Bush should immediately fire liberal Fran Townsend, former advisor to Janet Reno, who Robert Novak critiques in his 07/10/03 column titled, "Bush risks more damage from within." Novak says, "civil servants at Justice partially blamed [Fran Townsend] for the failure to investigate alleged September 11 terrorist Zacarias Moussaoui in time." Townsend advised Janet Reno, Novak says, essentially to "inhibit sharing of information between intelligence and prosecution which led to the failure to investigate Moussaoui's computer before September 11 which possibly could have prevented September 11." Fran Townsend should not be "the president's principal advisor on counter terrorism." We must get good people to be in charge of our intelligence and counter terrorism agencies and get rid of the bad ones. We also definitely need a complete overhaul of the State Department as well as the CIA and the FBI.

Getting back to Saddam and anthrax, a newspaper article published in the Birmingham News states that in 1983 the U.S. gave Saddam many biological weapons including the Ames strain of anthrax and West Nile virus! (I did not even realize West Nile virus was a biological weapon and that we gave it to Saddam until I read this article).

There is a very real possibility that al-Qaida terrorists introduced West Nile virus into this country. West Nile virus has now killed more than 286 people and

---

1. I have just learned today, June 3, 2004, as I am revising my first edition to update it, that George Tenet has resigned as director of the CIA. I do give him credit for telling President Bush there were WMD in Iraq, because there were WMD in Iraq until Saddam moved most of them to Syria and hid the rest in Iraq or destroyed them.

sickened over 4000. How easy it would be for a terrorist to inject ten rabbits with West Nile virus, and then place them in a mosquito-infested swamp and let the mosquitoes feed on them, thus introducing West Nile virus into the food chain. Think about it—how did a virus that is usually present in the Western Nile river region of Egypt suddenly cross miles of ocean and pop up in the state of New York? Now it has spread to the whole country. It is very possible this is thanks to Saddam and his al-Qaida buddies. And if any liberal foggy-headed nit wit journalist thinks there is no link between Saddam and international terrorists including al-Qaida, he needs his head examined.

The reason why the liberal media stuck its head in the sand and refused to print the evidence that Saddam did the anthrax attacks through terrorists is because the media did not want us to go to war against Iraq, partly because they are stupid and can't see the obvious danger that Saddam presented, partly because they are a bunch of overly pacifist wimps, and partly because they didn't want to see Bush and the Republicans win the war and get the well deserved credit they got for defending the security of America, after Clinton and Gore and the Democrats did nothing for the security of America, and indeed weakened it.

But let's get back to the Saddam—anthrax link. Remember that Saddam had thousands of warheads with anthrax at the end of the Gulf War, and that U.N. Inspectors could only account for 80% of them after the war. What happened to the other 20%? Saddam hid them and continue to grow anthrax.

The National Enquirer, and many other sources as well, reported that Mohammed Atta, the lead terrorist of September 11, was seen on four occasions meeting with Iraqi security agents prior to September 11—one of these meetings is well documented where he met in Prague and was observed by Czech security to leave a meeting with a top level Iraqi agent, and he was carrying two vials.

Next Mohammed Atta tried to buy a crop duster airplane in Belle Glade, Florida. Why did he want a crop duster airplane? To spread anthrax! Fortunately he was prevented from acquiring the crop duster plane by local authorities. Next, he was noted to have sought treatment for a suspicious bright red rash on his hands (anthrax lesions) at a local pharmacy in Boca Raton, Florida where he and his roommate lived[2]. (Not the roommate he had in Heidleberg, Germany who has been arrested, but the roommate he had in Boca Raton, Florida just prior to September 11.) That roommate is the person who sent the first anthrax letter in

---

2.   Time magazine also reported Atta's attempts to buy a crop duster airplane in Belle Glade, Florida and his seeking treatment for the rash on his hands, thus bolstering the National Enquirer's report.

October 2001 that killed the photographer at the <u>Sun</u> tabloid in the American Media, Inc. building where <u>The National Enquirer</u> was also published, in Boca Raton, Florida.

So we gave Saddam <u>the Ames strain</u> of anthrax in 1983. This was the anthrax that showed up in <u>all the attacks</u>! He cultivated it, and had thousands of warheads full of it in the Gulf War. Although much of that anthrax was destroyed after the Gulf War by U.N. weapons inspectors, some of it remained in secret places in Iraq.

Saddam gave the anthrax to his top level Iraqi security agents who gave it to Mohammed Atta who gave it to his roommate and to his fellow September 11 hijackers who gave it to their roommates who mailed the letters from Trenton, New Jersey which caused the months-long evacuation of our Senate building, and the deaths of several Americans.

Mohammed Atta and his roommate lived in Boca Raton, Florida where the first letter was mailed which killed the photographer at the <u>Sun</u>, the sister paper to <u>The National Enquirer</u>, which had <u>just</u> published a very unflattering article about Osama bin Laden which stated that when Osama was a young man and a playboy in Beirut, before his hyper-religious days, he was rejected by an American woman who laughed at him because he has a genital abnormality. Is it a coincidence that American Media, Inc., home of the <u>Sun</u> and <u>The National Enquirer</u>, was the first place attacked by anthrax, just after they published an unflattering article about Osama bin Laden? I think not!

Many of the other hijackers of September 11 lived in Trenton, New Jersey where the anthrax letters that attacked our Senate buildings came from. The hijackers had given anthrax to their roommates, who mailed the letters to Senators Daschle and Leahy, and also to Tom Brokaw, and the letters were postmarked from Trenton, New Jersey. Then all the roommates melted away and disappeared back into the woodwork.

It is very obvious that Saddam gave anthrax to the terrorists who then mailed the letters.

And a future anthrax mail out could be much more damaging, if the terrorists put pinpricks in the letters so more anthrax could cross-contaminate <u>thousands</u> of letters. I debated whether to write about this possibility for fear the terrorists may read my book and learn to pin prick future anthrax letters, but I suspect they have already thought about this technique, and I feel it is best for the public to be warned and to realize this might happen. We are in danger because that anthrax is now in the hands of Syria. Al-Qaida could get anthrax and put it in air conditioning vents. It could do the same with sarin or VX nerve gas.

If only we could have swiftly moved into Iraq, instead of dilly-dallying for a month begging the U.N. to help us enforce their own resolutions, we would have found lots of anthrax and also chemical WMD, before Saddam sent them in 18-wheeler trailer trucks to Syria!

Now that we have won the initial phase of the war, it is imperative that we stay the course, destroy the terrorists, and win the peace. We must stabilize Iraq, and create a safe and secure environment. We must immediately mobilize part of the old Iraqi Army to help us stabilize Iraq. The middle and lower level soldiers were not the Republican Guard or Saddam's inner circle. They did not fight against us. Just like General George Patton used some middle and lower level Nazi Party Members to stabilize Germany after World War II, and like General Douglas McArthur used the Japanese police to stabilize Japan, we need to use the middle and lower level Iraqi army to stabilize Iraq. Once the Iraqi soldiers feel empowered to help be part of the new Iraq, they can quickly identify and capture terrorists. They can tell who is a terrorist much better than we can. A current member of the Iraqi governing council, and now Prime Minister, Iyad Allawi, has called for the recall of the disbanded Iraqi army to stabilize Iraq. We should heed his call at once. It should also be noted that the wise, shrewd, and effective Newt Gingrich also supports mobilizing the disbanded Iraqi army, as do columnists Joseph Galloway and Trudy Rubin. Right now, the middle and lower level Iraqi army soldiers feel disenfranchised since they have lost their jobs and are now unemployed. Right now they have no motivation to help the U.S. find and capture the terrorists who are devastating Iraq. But if we mobilize them to help us stabilize Iraq, and give them jobs in the new security force, and pay them as much as we pay the Iraqi police force, so they can support their families, they will be strongly motivated to help us weed out terrorists and stabilize Iraq. This is the answer to the ongoing daily terror problem in Iraq! Also we need about 100,000 additional troops to first go in the Tribal areas of Northwest Pakistan, bordering Afghanistan, where Osama is hiding out, and get Osama, and stop him from funding terrorists in Pakistan, Kasmir, Afghanistan and Iraq, and after Osama is executed after a military tribunal, then the 100,000 troops need to come help out troops in Iraq to guard the hundreds of ammo dumps all over Iraq, so that the terrorists can't get weapons, and to guard the borders of Iran and Syria so they can't send in any more weapons or terrorists. I saw an American soldier inter-viewed on FOX TV eight months ago and he said we don't have enough troops to guard the hundreds and hundreds of ammo dumps Saddam set up all over Iraq. One of those ammo dumps is 9 miles by 9 miles—81 square miles!

We can't just blow up the ammo dumps whole—they have to be blown up little by little or else they will destroy the whole towns nearby.

I just can't believe the military planners at the Pentagon, Don Rumsfeld, and President Bush, and Congress, did not and <u>still</u> have not sent enough troops to guard the ammo dumps in Iraq! This is a <u>huge</u> military blunder! It is military beginner's class 101 that teaches that when you occupy a country, you guard any armories or weapons caches so the populace can't arm themselves. Now every Iraqi and his brother can just walk up to any of the hundreds of ammo dumps and pick up a rocket propelled grenade or an assault rifle or a mortar, or get a shell with which to make an explosive device! It is <u>common sense</u> that would say "Send enough troops to secure the ammo dumps!" Not to mention also sending enough troops to adequately guard the borders of Iraq with Syria and Iran so foreign terrorists can't flood into the country! Congress, the Administration, the Media, and the American people ought to be ashamed they didn't send, and still aren't sending, enough troops to do the job right.

The brilliant article, "A Proven Formula for How Many Troops We Need" [In Iraq], by Stephen Budiansky in the Sunday, May 9, 2004 <u>Washington Post</u> tells us <u>exactly</u> how to do the job right! Budiansky looks at history, and correctly observes the way we successfully occupied Germany after World War II, and also Kosovo in 1999, and applies it to the situation in Iraq.

He writes "The victors sent the right number to secure the peace in Germany after World War II, as well as to Kosovo in 1999. The number in Iraq isn't close to a realistic level."

He continues, "When Germany surrendered in May 1945, the U.S. Army had more than 1.6 million men within the borders of the defeated Nazi state."

"Army plans called for an occupation force of some 400,000 in the American zone for the first 18 months—or one U.S. soldier for every 40 Germans."

"In Iraq today, coalition forces number about 160,000, or one for every 160 Iraqis."

So we only have about <u>one-fourth</u> the troops we need in Iraq!

We need to send <u>at least</u> 100,000 troops, <u>NOW</u>, to first capture Osama, then quickly move into Iraq and guard the ammo dumps and secure the borders! If we also re-hire part of the old Iraqi Army, we could have Iraq stabilized in months! Then <u>finally</u>, we will stabilize Iraq and truly win the war <u>and</u> the peace. This way the Iraqi scientists will no longer fear Saddam nor his thugs and they can tell us about his nuclear program, his biological weapons program, and his chemical weapons program. Also the Baathist and al-Qaida thugs that are sniping at our troops will be left without a rallying point and a source of funds if Osama is con-

clusively killed or proved dead or captured. However we must also stop Syria and
Iran from sending terrorists to assassinate our troops. Recently newspapers
reported that Iran signed up 10,000 young men willing to be suicide bombers
and that the first wave has already been sent to Iraq. Iran wants to de-stabilize
Iraq so it can get control over Iraq. If we don't take these measures soon (recall
and mobilize the middle and lower level Iraqi Army as a police force, and send
100,000 more American troops to guard the ammo dumps and guard the Iran
and Syria borders to keep out al-Qaida fighters), the terrorists will escalate and
may blow up an entire army barracks like when suicide bombers killed 241 of our
Marines in Lebanon in 1983, or may hit a military transport plane with a Stinger
missile and kill hundreds of our troops. If the situation in Iraq is not dramatically
turned around soon I believe large scale terrorist attacks are inevitable. And when
they occur, not only will it be a terrible tragedy for our troops and their families,
it will also greatly increase the call to bring home our troops and abandon Iraq,
which would be a huge mistake since the terrorists would take over Iraq and use
its oil to fund the al-Qaida world-wide war of terror. Iraq would become, as
Turkish authorities put it, "a paradise for terrorists."

And even if President Bush and the Republicans and the good Democrats
(there are some good Democrats, like Senator Zell Miller) stand tough and don't
let the bad Democrats (the Wimpocrats) and the media pull our troops out of
Iraq, it may be for nothing if larger numbers of our troops are killed and maimed
by terrorists because it may cause President Bush to be defeated in 2004 and the
Republicans to lose their majority, and the Democrats will cut and run from Iraq
and we will lose not only the war in Iraq, but the global War on Terrorism. So it
is imperative for Bush and Rice and Rumsfeld to mobilize the Iraqi army and also
send in 100,000 more U.S. troops, so we can turn the situation around in Iraq
and win the war. And it is imperative for Bush to stay the course and truly stabilize Iraq and not try to get out too early for political reasons. Even a gradual "cut
and run" will be a disaster. We must stay the course.

God forbid that we elect the Big Flip-Flop, Hanoi John Kerry. He will for
sure pull us out of Iraq, and it will be the biggest disaster ever. Iraq will become a
terrorist paradise, funded by billions of dollars of Iraqi oil money, and America
and the world will be defeated in the War on Terror.

Now that we have captured Saddam, Bush's plan to turn him over for judgment to the new Iraqi government that will be formed this summer is a good one.
However, they must not let the terrorists spring Saddam out of jail. The current
plan is a good one, which is to keep Saddam under American military security,
while giving the Iraqis authority over him. I fear that if Saddam were under Iraqi

security only, he might escape. Saddam, and Osama, when he is caught, need to be tried and executed, so they won't come back on us.

We <u>don't</u> need to let the Europeans try Saddam in the Hague. They might give him one year, then probation.

When Osama bin Laden is caught, he needs to be tried by a <u>military tribunal on the spot</u> and he needs to be executed by a firing squad the moment he is found guilty. We <u>must</u> be tough and <u>kill terrorists</u> before they kill us.

I could not believe that President Bush, Colin Powell, and even Donald Rumsfeld were offering Saddam sanctuary in exile if he left Iraq before the war.

Here is the most dangerous, diabolical madman in the world since Hitler, a man with <u>billions</u> of dollars hidden in secret bank accounts all over the world, and they were going to let him go?

If Saddam hated America for driving him out of Kuwait in 1991, and took vengeance on America in the bombing of the World Trade Center in 1993, the destruction of the World Trade Center on September 11, 2001, the attack on the Pentagon September 11, and the attempted attack on the Capitol (Flight 93), and the anthrax attacks of October 2001, how much more would he hate America for kicking him out of his own country and taking his kingdom away from him? His hatred must be immense. And with his billions of dollars, he could wreak havoc on America by hiring his old hit-man Osama, and his terrorists, many of whom are sleeper agents right here in the U.S. The idea of letting Saddam go into exile was an incredibly stupid one, as stupid as the use of only two hundred American Special Forces troops in Afghanistan and the reliance on the unreliable Northern Alliance in the battle of Tora Bora, where we let Osama bin Laden slip away into Pakistan where he now sits in the lawless tribal area where the Pakistani government is afraid to go, plotting more terrorists attacks like the ones in Bali, Saudi Arabia and Kasmir, and Iraq and Afghanistan. If Osama succeeds in assassinating President Musharaff of Pakistan, as he has already tried to do twice in recent weeks, Islamic fundamentalists could take over Pakistan and give some of its nuclear weapons to al-Qaida. Osama <u>must</u> be stopped!

Geraldo Rivera never uttered truer words when he stated at the battle for Tora Bora, "It sure would be nice to see some U.S. Marines." But unfortunately all we had surrounding Osama bin Laden at Tora Bora, and surrounding Mullah Omar at Kandahar, were the Northern Alliance troops who quite understandably didn't want to risk a fight to the death with Osama or Omar and thus let them both escape, with hundreds of their men. My grandfather, General Hugh Cort, who was a general in World War II and who fought in many battles in Europe and the Pacific, always said, "You can't win a war with Air Force alone." If we had had

just 20,000 American troops on the ground, or less, we would have captured
Osama bin Laden at Tora Bora.

Geraldo Rivera gave the best on-site coverage of the war in Afghanistan. He
was right there at the front getting fired at, giving us via Fox news remarkable
views of Northern Alliance troops attempting to go up a mountain at Tora Bora
but having to retreat because of mortar fire from Osama's men. Where were all
the big anchors? I saw Dan Rather standing beside what looked like a big ware-
house in Kabul. I did not see him or any other journalist on the actual firing line
of the front of the War in Afghanistan except the brave Geraldo, always in the
action. Later, in the War in Iraq, many journalists did bravely follow Geraldo's
example and became embedded with the troops.

Now what we <u>have got to do</u> is get at least 50,000 troops or maybe 100,000
troops, by using some of the 42,000 U.S. troops presently in Japan and some of
the 300,000 U.S. troops presently in desk jobs in the U.S., and we need to <u>go
into Pakistan</u> and comb the 400 miles of caves on the Pakistan side of the
Afghanistan/Pakistan border and <u>find</u> Osama bin Laden. If the Pakistanis don't
like it, <u>too bad</u>! A few Special Forces guys might find Osama, or they might not,
but 50,000—100,000 troops <u>would find him</u>! And as soon as we find him, we
need to try him <u>on the spot</u> in a military tribunal and when we find him guilty
immediately execute him with a firing squad. And if the ACLU doesn't like it,
that is too bad for them. America needs to protect Americans from future terrorist attacks. We must do everything we can to prevent another September 11.

Chapter IV

✦

Future Terrorist Dangers, and Why This is Happening to America

We are facing terrible terrorist attacks and also terrible wars in the near future. Because of George W. Bush's and Tony Blair's great courage and history-making preemptive attack to destroy Saddam's regime <u>before</u> it got nuclear weapons, thus avoiding a nuclear World War III, America has been given a brief respite, a breather if you will. However, future dangers loom large. North Korea has nukes, and thanks to Bill Clinton, now has the missile technology to hit our cities on the West Coast with nuclear warheads. North Korea has been known to sell weapons to anyone and has been found to have given uranium to Libya (and remember when the Spaniards intercepted missiles going from North Korea to Yemen, and then the missiles were allowed to be delivered anyway, because a law against this had not yet taken effect, or some such nonsense, a few months prior to the war in Iraq?) North Korea has a million man army—we have seen videos of them goose-stepping like the Nazis through their square on the news. They have long wanted to take over South Korea, and they undoubtedly have missiles pointed at Seoul and also at our troops on the 38th parallel. They have a loose cannon for a leader, who might even be called a madman.

Then there is Iran—hot bed of Islamic terrorists, sponsor of Hizbollah and many other terrorist groups, soon to develop nuclear weapons.

There is Pakistan, already possessing nuclear weapons, a nation barely controlled by President Musharraf, with Osama bin Laden living in its borders, just on the Pakistan side of the Afghan-Pakistan border, and Osama is fomenting revolution, paying terrorists to kill Westerners in Karachi, and President Musharaff in Islamabad, and Indians in Kashmir, and our soldiers in Iraq and Afghanistan.

There is Syria, with headquarters for twenty-nine terrorist groups right in its capital of Damascus, which now probably are in control of many of Saddam's mobile biological weapons trailers that he sent to Syria just before the war in Iraq (the Israeli intelligence verifies that Saddam sent <u>convoys</u> of 18-wheeler truck trailers to Syria just before the Iraq War).

And the terrorists in the Bekka Valley of Lebanon, supported by Syria, are probably also in control of some of Saddam's chemical and biological weapons by now.

And there are several hundreds or thousands of al-Qaida sleeper terrorists living in America as we speak, getting ready to blow up bridges, national monuments, Congress, and other targets, and shoot down airplanes with Stinger missiles, and put bombs on commuter trains going through Penn Station underneath Madison Square Garden during the Republican Convention, and put anthrax or sarin in the convention hotels' air conditioning and ventilation systems, and crash airplanes into Times Square on New Year's Eve, and blow up the Super Bowl in January. And soon some of these terrorists will get hold of a suitcase nuclear bomb or two, and we will see horrible images of Manhattan and Washington going up in a nuclear blast, with mushroom clouds, despite all our best efforts.

And why has this come upon America, and what, if anything can be done about it?

Here is why we are in trouble—America has gotten so far away from God that we have gotten out from under His umbrella of protection.

We have <u>legalized</u> the horrible practice of abortion, where mothers get "physicians" to kill their own babies. We are keeping God out of our schools, and are giving kids condoms. We have taken the fatal step of calling homosexual relationships "marriage". Pat Robertson on CBN reports a <u>Washington Times</u> study with statistics showing that the average homosexual "marriage" lasts one and a half years, and during that time the partners have on average seven affairs. But even the rare monogamous gay "marriage" is unnatural and an aberration of nature. Every culture that has embraced homosexuality has been destroyed.

Now America, along with the Netherlands and Belgium, have become the first nations <u>in History</u> to ever legalize homosexual marriage! Not even Sodom and Gomorrah did this, and we see what happened to them! Marriage is a sacrament from God that joins a man and a woman. It is not for homosexuals. Child pornography is rampant on the Internet. 350,000 kids per year report that an adult has attempted to seduce them on the Internet. Children are being molested in department stores as their mothers shop in the next aisle. Drugs, homicide, kidnappings, robberies and all type of crime are everywhere—in small towns as well as in large urban areas. Suicide is a major cause of death among adolescents. And now we also face the danger of chemical, biological, and <u>nuclear</u> attacks from terrorists within, and nuclear attacks from rogue nations from without.

Pat Robertson and Jerry Falwell were absolutely right about America getting away from God and His protection and getting punished ever more severely by the forces of evil. Jerry Falwell apologized for his comments, but he should not have, because it is the truth. Pat Robertson did not back down, and he is right—America is being punished because of its departure from God, and, if America does not change and get back to God, it will eventually be destroyed.

The narrow election of the Godly leader, George W. Bush, has given our nation a brief reprieve. God sees President Bush and the Republicans and some Democrats enacting legislation to outlaw the unbelievably horrible practice of partial birth abortion, where a four to six month or even nine month old baby is pulled almost out of the womb, and then, without anesthesia, has scissors plunged into the base of its skull, and has its brains sucked out by a vacuum pump. There is no medical reason for this procedure—there is <u>never</u> a case where this procedure is necessary for the health of the mother—it is only done for the convenience of the mother and the abortionist.

For those who say abortion should be allowed in the case of rape, I say look at the wonderful life and ministry of the great evangelist James Robison, who was the product of rape. God uses him to save and feed thousands of starving people in Africa. Thank God his mother did not abort him! Clinton vetoed the ban on partial birth abortion bill twice, overruling the collective will of Congress and the American people (70% of Americans oppose partial birth abortion). But the Godly man George Bush signed the bill and America has outlawed partial birth abortion, which occurs about 3,000 times per year, and is neither rare nor necessary. For this good move that Congress has been making, God has given the U.S. partial victory in Afghanistan and Iraq. However, our victory is incomplete—Osama bin Laden still lives to wreak terror, and Iran and Syria and al-Qaida are sending terrorists into Iraq, and Baathist and Fedayeen terrorists are attacking us, and American soldiers are being killed and wounded every day in Iraq. And nuclear North Korea, and soon to be nuclear Iran lurk menacingly. And "sleeper" al-Qaida operatives live in our cities, waiting for their chance to kill thousands or even millions of us. Our very lives as Americans hang in the balance, as does our nation.

If we re-elect President Bush and not only continue the Republicans in majority in the Senate and House but <u>add</u> to it so we can overcome any Democratic filibusters, we have a fighting chance against terrorists and rogue nations, and crime and moral decay from within.

But if we, God forbid, elect a Democrat in 2004, or 2008, or 2012, we are doomed. As regards our National Defense, the Democrats can't beat their way out of a wet paper bag. They are committed to the abhorrent practice of abortion. A mother's womb ought to be the safest place in the world for a baby—but for over a million babies a year, it is the worst place to be, where their own mother asks an abortionist (not a doctor, because a true doctor would never do such a thing) to rip their arms and legs and head off with a forceps and then count the pieces afterward to make sure the limbs are all out. Even the first primitive doctors in ancient Greece knew abortion was wrong. In the Hippocratic Oath, which every doctor takes when graduating from medical school, it clearly states "Neither will I administer a poison for anybody when asked to do so, nor will I suggest such a course. Similarly I will not give to a woman a pressary to cause abortion." So why are we violating the Hippocratic Oath and killing thousands of unborn babies every day? And why are we killing our elderly with euthanasia in Oregon? In Holland, where euthanasia is wide-spread, thousands of elderly are killed every year without their consent! What is next? Are we going to be like the Nazis who killed over 200,000 handicapped people?

Our founding fathers would turn over in their graves if they knew the civil rights of unborn babies were being denied and that they were being killed in their mother's wombs. It is not enough to stop partial birth abortion—we must stop all abortion. Sav-a-life will help pregnant girls financially and medically to have their babies, and then either keep the baby or give it up for adoption to a good home. Why are we killing our babies, when there are couples waiting in line to adopt babies, and even going to foreign countries and paying thousands of dollars to adopt babies? For every couple that adopts a baby, there are a thousand on the waiting list that want to adopt a baby. But there aren't enough babies here in America to adopt because we are aborting them!

If America stops abortion, and turns from its many other sins, God will again bless America. But if America persists in abortion, and its other evils, God will bring upon America plague after plague, devastation after devastation, just as God brought the ten plagues on Egypt until finally Egypt let the Jewish people go free. In a similar way, God will bring plague after plague, disaster after disaster, on America until we either stop abortion, or finally be destroyed.

If you go to the Jefferson Memorial in Washington D.C. you will see, inscribed on the walls surrounding the statue of the great man, words that say, "Indeed I tremble for my country when I reflect that God is just, that His justice cannot sleep forever." Jefferson was talking about God's judgment that would come upon America in the Civil War for the abominable sin of slavery. These words can now also describe God's judgment that is coming upon America for the abominable sin of abortion. Jefferson also said, "God who gave us life gave us liberty. Can the liberties of a nation be secure when we have removed a conviction that these liberties are the gift of God?" If the Supreme Court rules that we must drop the words "one nation, under God" from the Pledge of Allegiance, it will be another sign of the beginning of the end of America.

I am really hoping for America to re-elect President Bush and the Republicans in 2004, 2008, and 2012 and beyond, so we can reverse the horrible downward death spiral that the liberal left Democratic leadership has taken us on.

But realistically, I fear that America will not heed these warnings. I despair that in 2004 or 2008 a Democrat will be elected President and the full decline and destruction of America will get underway.

I predict that if a Democrat president is elected in 2004 or 2008 and we do not overturn abortion, that we will see nuclear devastation come upon our country, either from within by terrorists living in our country or from without by rogue nations such as North Korea, Iran, and Syria. I fear we will see Manhattan destroyed, Washington D.C. destroyed, Boston destroyed, Chicago destroyed, and Los Angeles and many other of our cities destroyed and our country demoralized and dazed.

However, if that happens—and I truly hope it doesn't, but if it does—there is a glimmer of hope.

Chapter V

✦

The Cure

Here is the plan—elect a Republican super majority in the House and Senate, so any Democratic filibuster can be stopped. Re-elect George W. Bush in 2004, and then in 2008 elect a similarly dynamic Republican president, who will continue George W. Bush's heroic efforts but on an even larger and more dramatic scale. And I do mean dramatic. It is going to take dramatic <u>radical</u> change to save America. This President and Congress should overrule the Supreme Court on abortion. There is no way an unelected body of nine judges should decide a crucial issue for a nation such as abortion. This should be decided by a national referendum. And if Americans are truly educated about the horror that is abortion, if they are shown the mangled bodies of aborted babies on the news, if they see, as I have, video of a trash can behind an abortion clinic with the arms and legs of five and six month old babies hanging over the side, if they witness a partial birth abortion, and see the baby jerk out its arms and legs in agony when the abortionist plunges his scissors into the base of its skull, and hear the horrible sucking sound as the baby's brains are sucked down the vacuum tubing, and if they hear from mothers who have suffered physical and emotional pain for a lifetime from abortion, and if they review the medical facts about abortion (it is never necessary for the health of the mother, and in fact, abortion increases the chance of infertility and breast cancer in the mother), and if America is shown the true facts of abortion on TV (which the left wing liberal media won't show us now), America will vote to end abortion. And then God will bless us again, and give us victory against the terrorists and the nuclear rogue nations. We must also confirm that marriage is a sacrament from God that joins a man to a woman only, and is not for homosexuals. We must punish child molesters with a mandatory ten-year sentence without parole for a first offense, and twenty years without parole for each subsequent offense.

We will first try diplomacy in dealing with the following rogue nations, but if we do not achieve our goals with diplomacy we must use military force.

We will pressure North Korea to give up their nukes before they sell a nuke to al-Qaida or we will take out their nuclear facilities with strategic bombing, just like the Israelis took out Saddam's Osirik reactor in 1981. If they then invade South Korea, we must deal with them harshly. The Chinese will object, but if they dare to go to war against us, which is doubtful, since they desire our trade, we will defeat them. We will pressure Syria to destroy the terrorists there, and then clean up the terrorist mess of the Bekka Valley of Lebanon, or else we will do it ourselves with military force. We cannot allow Syria to let the terror groups headquartered there use Saddam's biological and chemical weapons against us. Then we will stop Iran's nuclear program, either diplomatically or by military force. We will send 100,000 or more troops to comb the caves of Western Pakistan until we find Osama bin Laden and execute him after a military tribunal. We will then send those 100,000 troops to Iraq and truly stabilize Iraq. We will arrest Yasser Arafat and try him in a military tribunal and when he is found guilty execute him for giving the orders that killed our diplomats in 1973 and for signing invoices to pay for chemicals for suicide bombers recently in Israel.

Iran is a <u>huge</u> danger to America. At the end of June 2004 the United States expelled two Iranian security guards at Iran's U.N. mission for surveilling and videotaping a variety of New York City landmarks and infrastructures. The Iranians had been caught doing this <u>two times</u> previously and had been warned by the U.S. to stop.

This is <u>very alarming</u>. Iran wants to de-stabilize Iraq so it can gain control of Iraq. I believe Iran was surveilling New York City landmarks and infrastructures in order to have terrorists hit the city during the Republican convention! They are trying, along with al-Qaida, to do a big terrorist attack on New York City before the presidential election just like al-Qaida did in the Madrid commuter train bombings in Spain, in an attempt to scare the American people into voting for Kerry, who would probably pull us out of Iraq. However the American people, unlike the Spanish people who were intimidated into voting for a pacifist leader who is pulling them out of Iraq, will <u>not</u> be intimidated. In fact, if the Iranians and al-Qaida hit New York City, it will anger Americans and they will re-elect George W. Bush, who, unlike John Kerry will go after and destroy terrorists.

So it is vital that we do not be fooled by Iran into thinking that they are only developing peaceful nuclear power. An oil-rich country like Iran does not even need peaceful nuclear power for its energy needs. They are developing nuclear bombs, and have already enriched uranium and re-processed plutonium, two of the most important steps for making a nuclear weapon, and will give them to terrorists to blow up our cities. We <u>must truly</u> force them to give up their nuclear weapon development program, or we <u>must</u> take it out with military force.

If we do not stop Iran's nuclear weapons program, our cities are doomed to destruction. So we will stop their nuclear weapons program, either diplomatically or by military force, and possibly even help the good Iranian people who favor a democracy to overthrow the Mullahs.

We will crush the state sponsors of terrorism, and then we will crush the terrorists in Palestine.

Then we will set up true democracies in each nation that we clean up, just like we did in Japan and Germany after World War II.

We will honor God, and we will follow His precepts. And then God will bless us, and our children, and our children's children.

God bless America and America bless God!

Post Script

An Open Letter to President Bush

Dear Mr. President,

You and Tony Blair are heroes for preemptively taking out Saddam before he got nukes and could give them to terrorists. You have saved America from having its cities blown up by terrorists with nuclear bombs.

You will go down in history as the man who saved America. However, all this will be for nothing, and your glory will be sullied forever, and America will lose the global War Against Terror, if you do not win the peace in Iraq as well as the initial war.

If you get out of Iraq prematurely, in response to political or media or budget pressures, and do not adequately stabilize Iraq, the consequences will be <u>far far</u> worse than Kennedy's cowardly pulling back U.S. air support in the Bay of Pigs, which resulted in 3000 brave Cuban Americans being slaughtered or captured and tortured by Castro, or your father's grave mistake of encouraging the Shi'ites and the Kurds to rise up against Saddam after the Gulf War, and then leaving them to be slaughtered by Saddam, even as our helicopters hovered overhead, doing nothing.

No, President Bush, if you let anything get you out of Iraq too soon, if you turn over Iraq to the Iraqis and leave without continuing to ensure stability with U.S. troops, you will open up Iraq to the greatest blood bath imaginable. After the Shi'ites slaughter the Sunnis and vice versa, and after the Iranians and al-Qaida take over Iraq, it will be a terrorist paradise. If we didn't like al-Qaida in Afghanistan, think what it would be like to have al-Qaida in Iraq with access to ten billion dollars a year in oil revenues! We need to stay in Iraq like we stayed in Germany and Japan, at least 5 years, to <u>truly</u> stabilize it, whatever the cost. And you and your advisors don't need to be talking about <u>reducing</u> troop strength; you need to <u>add</u> troop strength to turn this terrorism situation around in Iraq.

Here is how you can win the peace in Iraq—send 100,000 <u>additional</u> troops, <u>whatever the cost</u>, to Pakistan at the border of Afghanistan and search those 400 miles of caves and <u>find</u> Osama bin Laden, because he is funding a lot of the terrorism against our troops in Iraq and Afghanistan. Then as soon as we find him and hold a military tribunal and execute bin Laden, send the 100,000 troops to Iraq to guard all the ammo dumps in Iraq and to guard the Iran and Syria borders to stop Iran and Syria from sending in weapons and terrorists.

And <u>please</u>, for the sake of our brave soldiers, <u>spend the money</u> to get them <u>all</u> interceptor body armor (Kevlar vests) so they will be properly protected. It is an outrage that they don't have them already. Don't try to win this war on the cheap—spend <u>whatever it takes</u> and <u>do it right</u>!

Also, <u>immediately</u>, recall and mobilize part of the old Iraqi army and enlist them to help the Iraqi police to weed out and capture and kill the terrorists that are attacking our troops and moderate Iraqis. And please pay them the same salary as the Iraqi police, so they can support their families. This should have been done right from the beginning. Once the Iraq army soldiers see they will get jobs, they will help us destroy the terrorists. Then the terrorism will soon stop, stability will be achieved, and Iraq, like Japan and Germany, will be a stable country and not a terrorist heaven. Do this now, <u>whatever</u> it costs. It is better to go ahead and spend more money, send more troops, hire more former Iraqi army soldiers, whatever it takes, to <u>do the job right</u> and win the peace in Iraq so our soldiers will be safe and Iraq will be secure. Do this now, before we lose 300 troops in a Beirut-like car bomb, or lose 300 troops when a military transport jet gets shot down by a Stinger missile; act now before it's too late!

Also, when you hopefully get re-elected in November, you <u>must</u> tackle the problems of Iran getting nuclear weapons and North Korea already having nuclear weapons. You need to first do everything you can diplomatically to truly take away their nuclear weapons programs, and if that fails you <u>must</u> take out their nuclear capability with military force. Then you must pressure Syria to truly wipe out the terrorists in Syria and Lebanon, and since they probably won't comply you will probably have to accomplish this with military force, in order to destroy the chemical and biological weapons that Saddam sent there. Then you must consider taking away Pakistan's nuclear weapons, and you must prevent even peaceful small countries like Brazil from getting enriched uranium capability, because al-Qaida could possibly get hold of weapons grade uranium. And you must always defend Israel from the many countries that want to destroy Israel. God says in the Bible that He will bless those who bless Israel.

And you must not only appoint good judges to the Supreme Court who are for life and not for abortion (don't be fooled like your father was by David Souter), but you must also bring about an amendment to the Constitution protecting the lives of all unborn children, and stopping all abortion. And you must pass the amendment stating marriage is between a man and a woman only.

Then God will truly bless America, and we will finally be safe from terrorists.

This is a tall order for your next four years, Mr. President, but you are a great man of God, chosen by God, and with God's help you, and Congress, and the American people can accomplish it!

0-595-31585-2